HOLLYWOOD LEGENDS

HOLLYWOOD LEGENDS: 'LIVE' ON STAGE

MARLENE
by Pam Gems

OBEDIENTLY YOURS, ORSON WELLES
by Richard France

JAMES DEAN IS DEAD!
(LONG LIVE JAMES DEAN)
by Jackie Skarvellis

Introduced by Simon Callow

OBERON BOOKS
LONDON

First published in this collection in 2011 by Oberon Books Ltd
521 Caledonian Road, London N7 9RH
Tel: 020 7607 3637 / Fax: 020 7607 3629
e-mail: info@oberonbooks.com
www.oberonbooks.com

Contents

INTRODUCTION
by Simon Callow   7

MARLENE
by Pam Gems   11

OBEDIENTLY YOURS, ORSON WELLES
by Richard France   63

JAMES DEAN IS DEAD! (LONG LIVE JAMES DEAN)
by Jackie Skarvellis   143

Introduction

A remarkably large number of plays are named after their central characters, but, until recent times, they have rarely been portraits of those characters, being rather dramas driven by or evolving from those characters. *Richard III, John Gabriel Borkman, Uncle Vanya*, are none of them biographical plays as such. The biographical play first emerged in the nineteenth century. The Victorians' increasing fascination with historiography led to the (generally somewhat idealised) recreation of earlier periods, in both painting and in the theatre. Figures like Charles I featured heavily, appealing as he did to contemporary notions of doomed nobility; great attention was paid to researching the exact appearance and the gestures and customs of the time. In the twentieth century, a school of playwriting sprang up of which the English verse playwright John Drinkwater was the most prominent: his subjects included Oliver Cromwell, Robert Burns, and, most famously, Abraham Lincoln; there were innumerable biographical plays about Shakespeare, Socrates, Handel, and one, sensational in its defiance of the Lord Chamberlain, about Oscar Wilde. After the war, plays about Thomas More, Mary Stuart, Martin Luther, Henry II (twice – once by Jean Anouilh, the second time by James Goldman), were among the most successful commercial plays of the period; while somewhat more controversial works about Winston Churchill, J. Robert Oppenheimer and Pope Pius XII were to be found in the subsidised theatre. For the most part these plays are interested in their central characters as historical figures, people who actually lived: the plays, even the political ones among them, strive to convey what they were like and why they did what they did, as opposed to seeing them as symbolic and representative figures in the way that Tamburlaine, say, is. The plays are interested in individuals as such.

A parallel development was the great upsurge of biographical films in the thirties and forties, in which revolutionaries like Juárez, writers like Zola and great scientists like Pasteur and Marie Curie were portrayed: Paul Muni made a bit of a career out of this sort of thing. What has been apparent from the early years of the twentieth century is that biographical theatre offers opportunities for an actor, and perhaps especially for a solo actor, or a lightly supported solo actor, that are immense. The public is always fascinated by biography – by the trajectory of a human life – especially if it ends in catastrophe. It is the same impulse that draws many of us to turn first to the obituary pages of the newspapers: how did this or that prominent representative of the human race make use of the set of cards fate dealt him or her? This curiosity is particularly sharp in the case of the prodigiously endowed: those who are uncommonly beautiful, gifted, brainy. There is, I suspect, a certain *schadenfreude* in contemplating the wreck of greatness.

The method of making theatre out of the individuals in question varies widely. I have, rather to my surprise, made a bit of a speciality of playing people who actually lived. My first essay in the genre was the Roman poet Juvenal, about whose physical appearance and personal tics we have next to no information, so my carte for that was fairly blanche; Peter Shaffer's Mozart I was able to make quite a good fist of with the aid of paintings and people's memoirs; with Jean-Jacques Rousseau, the pioneer of modern autobiography, we had almost too much information. Later I played Verlaine on stage in Christopher Hampton's masterly *Total Eclipse,* again closely relying on documentary evidence; on screen I played Emanuel Schikaneder, Richard Cosway, Charles Dickens, all as realistically as possible. Film is largely a realistic medium; in time, I came to feel that on stage I wanted to try something more impressionistic by way of evocation, and I found my model in Micheál MacLiammóir's Oscar Wilde play *The Importance of Being Oscar,* a brilliant solution to a practical problem: the slight and medium-sized MacLiammóir bore no physical resemblance to his subject, who was almost a giant. MacLiammóir's approach was to talk about Wilde, to inhabit his characters, and only gradually to begin to speak in his voice, so that a picture of Wilde was built up by suggestion in the audience's head. I have subsequently appeared in two other plays based on that matrix, Peter Ackroyd's *The Mystery of Charles Dickens* and Jonathan Bate's *The Man from Stratford*, which have been deeply satisfying to perform, making the audience active rather than passive, which was a difficulty I had experienced with a number of solo shows by very distinguished performers – Henry Fonda as Clarence Darrow and James Earl Jones as Paul Robeson – who addressed us directly in character. There has, it seems to me, to be a dramatic relationship between the character and the audience; there need to be points of tension and obstacles as in any play.

The plays in this volume all deal with performers, which is a very obviously appealing idea, since the element of performance can add a metaphysical dimension. The three plays are very different from each other in concept and tone – as different, indeed, as their three subjects, though Marlene and Orson of course knew each other well, and it is hard to imagine neither being interested in the dangerous and fitfully brilliant boy from Indiana. What he might have thought of *them*, of course, is another matter. I can vouch for the absolute authenticity of one of the plays, Richard France's *Obediently Yours, Orson Welles*, written by a pioneering Welles scholar, but what matters is the theatrical instinct, which all three possess in spades. To convey the essence of a human being, to show him or her in action, so that by the end of the evening you feel that you have spent privileged time in their company, is quite an achievement, requiring no little cunning on the part of the author; when it comes off, it constitutes one of the quintessential acts of theatre: that the audience is different when they walk out of the auditorium from the way they were when they walked in.

Simon Callow, September 2010

MARLENE

By Pam Gems

INTRODUCTION

Pam Gems

I suppose mine was the first generation – in the twenties – to grow up with the movies as an integral part of life. We didn't stop reading, anything up to four books at a time, twice weekly from the town library. But this fodder for mind, heart and soul was supported by three times a week to the local Regent Cinema.

Programmes ran Monday, Tuesday, Wednesday, all change for Thursday, Friday, Saturday and a completely new menu on Sunday. Saturday mornings were reserved for children, with a serial. And programmes were programmes then... Each contained a major feature, 'B' feature, newsreel, cartoon and short. Programmes were continuous and interrupted constantly by stentorian calls of 'Is this where we came in?' and the thwack of seats going up. An aged aunt arrived at midday, and, for her sixpenny ticket (she preferred the front row) stayed put until *The King* was played at ten thirty. She was respected as an expert, knowing the names of all the character actors... Elisha Cook, S.Z. 'Cuddles' Zakall, and Maria Ouspenskaya. The rest of us stuck with the stars. We were the stars. Blundering out into the high street from Malibu, Old Vienna or 42nd Street, you found yourself walking high-shouldered like Joan, or tossing curls like Ginger. How can we say that we aren't imbued, infected by it all? That our lives have not been modified by early and constant exposure to movies. The first time I saw *El Paso*, it was like coming home. Human beings live and learn by imprinting, as any good teacher knows. Yell at them to be quiet and you are teaching them how to yell. We model ourselves on the patterns around us... Mr Nice Guy Kevin Costner... Mr Cheeky Nice Guy Mel Gibson... Mr Anarchic Nice Guy Harrison Ford... Mr Wimpy Nice

Guy Tom Hanks. But what about the women? The female models? Where are they? The Siren – the Madonna – the Girl Next Door – the Femme Fatale? Not where they were. Except of course for Marlene Dietrich.

In the thirties and forties, the all-powerful Hollywood studios created many female stars, from the *fatale* to the *soubrette*. Goddesses for all occasions. They had the pick of the world's beautiful women to choose from. And they picked Dietrich. Together with the incomparable Garbo, the delicious Myrna Loy, and great beauties... Hedy Lamarr, Joan Bennett, Vivien Leigh, Rita Hayworth. Many were better actresses than Marlene, as she herself was always the first to pronounce. An intelligent, educated woman (she was trained to be a concert violinist) she knew the score. That what was required from her was not acting in the traditional sense – but being. For the camera. Being an image as evanescent as smoke. Beauty, like smoke, is fragile. And impermanent. Except that Marlene was a German, a Junker's daughter – and a stayer. A rarity in a metier of constant casualty, reject and turnover. Someone, talking to Hollywood movie director George Cukor, made a disparaging remark about movie actresses. Their vapidity, tantrums, concern with looks, hair, I don't know. Cukor turned on him. They were all, he said, heroines. To survive in that world, to be a movie star and female, took the greatest fortitude, ingenuity, toughness of spirit. Heroines, he insisted. But most of them, alas, box office poison by their mid-thirties.

By that time for Marlene we were at war with Germany. And Marlene was German, although a naturalised American... a Berliner. Goebbels had tried desperately to lure her back to Germany in the thirties 'to head the film industry of our glorious Reich'. Instead, Marlene went into uniform and entertained Allied troops all over the world, going into battle zones in Europe where, if the Germans had caught her, they would have strung her up with piano wire... resentment against her in Germany persist to this day. She was a brave woman. After the war she made a few more movies and then became a cabaret and concert performer. And an icon of a singular nature. Marlene does not belong to the more familiar category of victim-icon. She is no Judy... no Marilyn, beseeching us with husky voice and terrified eyes. There is none of that pulsating empathy with the vulnerable, the threatened within us. With Marlene there was of course the beauty, the Nordic colouring, the incomparable cheekbones, the legs. But by the great years of her touring as a solo performer, we knew that to be an illusion. What stood before us onstage was memory, transience. And yet. Here she was, as lovely as ever, singing the same songs, those songs we had heard when the bombs were falling, when we wrote those letters, wondering if he would get them, whether he was still alive. Yet our icon did not console. She kept herself to herself. She judged us. She accepted our worship... demanded it, turned it over for worth. And bowed acceptance. This icon was Aphrodite and Diana, Juno and Demeter in one. In her private life Dietrich was known to be a lasting and loyal friend, staunch if you were ill or in distress. She had many dependents. She worked, as she said in print, because she needed the money. And because she needed us. As we need her. A modern icon. A made woman. A stayer. Tough, hard to please, alluring, comforting... and there for us. The working Madonna.

Pam Gems

Characters

MARLENE DIETRICH

VIVIAN HOFFMAN

MUTTI

MUSICIANS
(Piano, Violin, Double Bass)

Songs

YOU GO TO MY HEAD – Coots/Gillespie
(B. Feldman & Co., c/o EMI Music Publishing Ltd.)

YOU DO SOMETHING TO ME – C. Porter
(Chappell Music Ltd., c/o Warner/Chappell Music Ltd.)

LOOK ME OVER CLOSELY – T. Gilkyson
(Montclare Music Ltd., c/o Music Sales Ltd.)

ILLUSIONS – F. Hollaender
(Famous Music Group)

I WISH YOU LOVE – C. Trenet/A. Beach
(EMI Virgin Music Ltd., c/o EMI Music Publishing Ltd.)

NAUGHTY LOLA – F. Hollaender
(Campbell Connelly, c/o Music Sales Ltd.)

MEIN BLONDES BABY – P. Kreuder/F. Rotter
(Ralph Maria Siegel Muzik Edition, Nachfolger GmbH & Co.)

LIEBE OHNE LIEBE – G.E. Lessing
(public domain work)

JONNY – F. Hollaender
(Chappell Music Ltd., c/o Warner/Chappell Music Ltd.)

WARUM – Stolz/Reisch/Robinson
(Campbell Connelly, c/o Music Sales Ltd.)

THE LAZIEST GIRL IN TOWN – C. Porter
(Chappell Music Ltd., c/o Warner/Chappell Music Ltd.)

SEE WHAT THE BOYS IN THE BACK ROOM WILL HAVE
F. Hollaender/F. Loesser
(EMI United Partnership Ltd., c/o EMI Music Publishing Ltd.)

MAKIN' WHOOPEE – Kahn/Donaldson
(EMI Music Publishing Ltd.)

LILI MARLENE – Schultz/Leip/Connor/Phillip
(Peter Maurice Music Co. Ltd., c/o EMI Music Publishing Ltd.)

HONEYSUCKLE ROSE – Waller/Razaf
(Memory Lane Music Ltd. & Redwood Music Ltd.)

WHERE HAVE ALL THE FLOWERS GONE – Pete Seeger
(Harmony & Fall River Music Inc., c/o Bucks Music Group)

LA VIE EN ROSE – Piaf/Louiguy
(Noel Gay Music Co. Ltd.)

FALLING IN LOVE AGAIN – F. Hollaender/Connelly
(Campbell Connelly, c/o Music Sales Ltd.)

Marlene was first performed at the Oldham Coliseum Theatre on 2nd October 1996 with the following cast:

MARLENE Siân Phillips

VIVIAN HOFFMAN Lou Gish

MUTTI Billy Mathias

MUSICIANS: PIANO Kevin Amos

VIOLIN Julian Jackson

Director Sean Mathias

Musical direction and incidental music Kevin Amos

Designer Michael Vale

Costumes Terry Parsons

Lighting Mark Jonathan

Sound Clement Rawling

Assistant Director Thierry Harcourt

The play then opened at the Lyric Theatre, Shaftesbury Avenue, London, on 8th April 1997 with the following change:

MUSICIANS: PIANO Kevin Amos

VIOLIN Julian Jackson

DOUBLE BASS John Richards

The play is set in Paris in the 1970s.

ACT ONE

MARLENE's dressing room. It is well-appointed. Wrapped flowers in buckets.

Onstage, VIVIAN HOFFMAN, awaiting MARLENE's arrival. She is in her thirties, narrow-faced with short hair. She wears a man-tailored suit, plain blouse, a man's watch and good shoes. Her manner is tense and expectant. MUTTI, an elderly woman who looks like a cross between a refugee and a concierge, appears briefly, goes away, returns and wanders off. She seems confused. Over the loudspeaker there are sounds of workmen, music and voices. Then through the mêlée the voice of the STAGE MANAGER cuts in:

STAGE MANAGER: Tout le monde... everyone... clear the corridors, please. I want those corridors clear – now. Miss Dietrich will be here any minute. I repeat Miss Dietrich will be here any minute. Wardrobe staff to the stage door, please, to greet Miss Dietrich. Are there fans at the stage door?

GISELLE: Oui M'sieu.

STAGE MANAGER: How many?

GISELLE: A lot – I arranged big crowd.

STAGE MANAGER: Good. Are those corridors clear? We don't want an accident. Isolde... I want you at the top of the steps. The house manager will be at the bottom to welcome Miss Dietrich, be en garde at the top.

ISOLDE: D'accord...

STAGE MANAGER: Giselle, are you in place?

MUTTI crosses and exits.

GISELLE: Oui m'sieu... sommes là.

STAGE MANAGER: OK bravo, tout le monde... what? Yes, yes! Oui? Tout le monde, Miss Dietrich has arrived.

VIVIAN exits quickly.

I repeat Miss Dietrich has arrived. Keep those corridors clear. Where is she? – Music... play the music!

A burst of 'The Blue Danube', played too fast, bursts out of the loudspeaker. MARLENE enters through the auditorium. Music is lowered.

MARLENE: (*Calling back, waving someone away.*) Go away... you can't find something better to do than ask stupid questions? 'Did you have a good trip?!' Is Bismarck a herring? (*Arriving onstage, calls.*) And tell them to turn off that verdammt music! Why are they playing *The Blue Danube*? I am not Owstwian, who do they think I am – Hitler? All this toodle toodle toodle...

She looks around.

My God, what have they done? The gweatest little whorehouse in Texas! Who are they trying to impress?

She shakes her head, repressing a smile, and walks down to the footlights, not displeased with the fuss made for her. She looks up and around at the lights.

Mmm – new rig?

She looks out at the auditorium, and up at the circle and the gods.

Well... here I am. Yah – it's me. And don't think I'm afraid of you!

She moves about, tries for sound, singing a few lines of 'YOU GO TO MY HEAD'. *

Yah – OK – right. Now a small whisky to face the hideous filth and smell of sepulchre backstage – V! You're here! You made it!

* For copyright details on the songs used in the stage production of *MARLENE*, please consult the list on pages 18-19.

VIVIAN enters.

You made it!

They embrace.

VIVIAN: We were all at the stage door to greet you – !

MARLENE: Waste of energy, I came by the box office –
let me look at you. You're here!

VIVIAN: Of course I'm here.

MARLENE: Only I wasn't sure. Alex thought you might
be in production –

VIVIAN: Put the coat away, you knew I'd come.

MARLENE: Thank you sweetheart – no, I mean it.
(*Casually.*) You got my cables?

VIVIAN: All fifteen of them.

MARLENE: And?

VIVIAN: Everything's covered – so they say.

MARLENE: (*Darkly.*) Time will tell.

VIVIAN: (*Consulting her notes.*) I don't *think* we've messed
up –

MARLENE: Of course you haven't – I'm so grateful
you're doing this for me.

VIVIAN: What are friends for? (*Pours drinks.*)

MARLENE: I can't have strangers in the dressing room,
you know that, V.

VIVIAN: I'm flattered you asked me.

MARLENE: Both the Onassis sisters out of town, the Dutch
princess pregnant, I was even down to Dolores!

VIVIAN puts down her drink, deflated.

MARLENE: My God, that woman. Sits in Romanoffs in
a hat that keeps hitting you in the face – promises,

promises, then a call, would you believe from Alaska?
She's on a mercy errand. Which I would have
believed but for the reggae music in the back.

VIVIAN: Dolores, huh?

MARLENE notices VIVIAN's glum expression.

MARLENE: Sweetheart – baby – normally I wouldn't
DARE to ask you – I only asked Dolores because –
listen, this is a woman who wears white to her own
daughter's wedding!

VIVIAN: I heard she served chilli to the Pope.

MARLENE: Hah!

VIVIAN: No doubt some grim, Polish recipe –

MARLENE: Did the trunks arrive?

VIVIAN: Finally, after we threatened all-out nuclear
attack. I was on the phone through the night.

MARLENE: So everything is in order?

VIVIAN: Checked and arranged as per your instructions.

MARLENE: No damage?

VIVIAN: One shoulder-strap, already mended.

MARLENE: Oh V, you're going to be such a help!

VIVIAN: I hope so. Just tell me what you need, and be
gentle – I haven't done this before.

MARLENE: You'll be fine.

VIVIAN: I'd hate to mess up for you.

MARLENE: We'll have a great time. I'm so easy... you
can't do these international tours if you're not
relaxed... you must be easy, easy, easy...

VIVIAN: Save the energy for the performance, you
mean?

MARLENE: You see? You understand so well. Just relax, sweetheart. (*Clicks her fingers.*) Messages?

VIVIAN: (*Fumbles, produces them, gives them to MARLENE and reads from nine loose pieces of paper.*) Two calls from Yul Brynner... best wishes from Ingrid and Princess Margaret... a beautiful posy of red roses from Jean Gabin...

MARLENE: (*Murmurs.*) Ah – Jean... he never forgets... (*Kisses her fingers to him.*)

VIVIAN: ... a jar of honey from Charles Aznavour.

MARLENE: The dear boy.

VIVIAN: ... and do you want a free mink if you model it?

MARLENE: No, what's wrong with sable? (*Reading her messages murmurs, throwing away messages.*) No... No... oh, a message from Picasso... no... (*Reading the next.*) Ahh... from Président Pompidou. The dear man has a shy pancreas! Ring the homeopath behind the Rue Saint-Honoré, the number is in my green book. Oh – tell the hotel where the band is staying, good Scottish T-bone steaks please, no porterhouse or rump – I want those boys in good shape – and send some fraises des bois – strawberries – to Princess Grace, they've had a crop failure. (*Getting the Hoover.*) How's the Box Office?

VIVIAN bends picking up the discarded messages, shouts over the sound of the Hoover.

VIVIAN: Sell out!

MARLENE: Yah?

VIVIAN: Queues around the block for returns. Marlene, that is absolutely unnecessary. They assure me everything's been spring-cleaned, not to mention completely redecorated.

MARLENE: Yah, three shows ago. Listen, I am not new with theatre managements.

VIVIAN: They sent you the paint samples!

MARLENE: I know for a fact the last performer in this dressing room had syphilis.

VIVIAN: A mild case of hepatitis, they assured me.

MARLENE: (*Sarcastic.*) Oh – well!
And where is my water?

VIVIAN: They're getting it.

MARLENE: Thank you sweetheart.

VIVIAN: (*Picks up a large old tin box, painted khaki with a large red cross painted on the side.*) This looks battle worn.

MARLENE: That's because it's been around. Like me.

VIVIAN: A box with a past!

MARLENE: You could say so.

They laugh. She looks at the box, a moment of reverie.

I'll never forget...

VIVIAN: (*Eager for reminiscence from MARLENE.*) Yes?

MARLENE: Italy... 1944. Making love in the back of a two-ton truck with a young G.I. I needed the medicine box after that, believe me.

VIVIAN: Comfort for the troops?

MARLENE: Why not? (*Shrugs, seemingly detached.*) Most of that unit was wiped out... Oh, it's good to have you here! This tour has been so lonely... in the dressing room only Mutti, and you can't talk to *her.*

VIVIAN: Hardly. Well – I'm here and you're looking wonderful.

MARLENE: Oh please.

VIVIAN: How are the legs?

MARLENE: Legendary. Where is my water?

VIVIAN: They're getting it!

MARLENE: (*Growls.*) Quicker I make it myself. (*Sees the flowers.*) That damn woman – she did it again! Where is she? Mutti! Mutti!! Wrong – wrong – wrong – well, how can she know, she's only been with me twenty years!

MUTTI appears timidly. MARLENE points accusingly at the flowers.

I said to buy different bouquets from different florists! These are all exactly the same. They are in the same wrap! Now I must rearrange! (*To VIVIAN.*) They are for the usherettes to present at the end of the show – I'll explain later – (*Shouts at MUTTI.*) – the whole thing you give away – she wants to shame me – show me up!

MUTTI, stricken, comes forward to take the flowers.

No... I don't listen... go – (*Waving MUTTI off.*) You are fired – she is fired.

MUTTI goes.

VIVIAN: Leave them to me, I'll see to them.

MARLENE: My only reliable friend.

VIVIAN: Now that's not true. Marlene – (*Points offstage.*) – did that woman never speak?

MARLENE: Mutti? (*Curt.*) Since Dachau? No.

VIVIAN picks up the flowers.

Thank you sweetheart.

VIVIAN: Ah, I nearly forgot, Ginette Spanier is arranging a party for you to meet everyone in town. Rubenstein is playing at the British Embassy, he says he won't start until you get there!... and Noël Coward arrives tomorrow!

MARLENE: Wonderful. Oh – don't forget – it's *Sir* Noël now – we don't want a fatality.

VIVIAN: (*Laughs.*) Please – I'm too young to die!

She smiles, clutching the flower bucket, and goes.

MARLENE: Yah. (*She catches sight of herself in the glass.*) Gott im Himmel. This glass is so old!

(*She pulls a face at herself in the glass.*) We deal with you later. First things first – (*She looks round and yells.*) Water!!

VIVIAN runs on with a pail of water, plonks the pail before MARLENE, produces a pair of garish rubber gloves and presents them to MARLENE with mock formality. MARLENE puts on the gloves, looks around for something to kneel on, to VIVIAN's amusement uses a fur jacket. VIVIAN watches, amazed, as MARLENE, kneeling on the fur, begins to clean the floor efficiently. Sounds on the PA.

MARLENE: Thank you sweetie, OK, go now and turn off that damn noise!

VIVIAN waves a placating hand, switches off the sound in the dressing room, goes.

MARLENE: They have no idea. 'Oh, Miss Dietrich! Welcome to Rio, London, Sydney! SO good to see you again!' (*Sotto voce.*) 'Look at her – fifth world tour!... schlepping around the world and back again – what for?' 'Oh, you know, these old movie stars, it's like a drug to them... they need the applause.'

Like hell.

I need the money. (*Shrugs.*) AND the applause.

Now Paris. The only city for a woman. Yah, but for Paris you must be wonderful. Wonderful? After ten hours on a plane eating purple food, ankles swollen and not seeing so good? I need oxygen! Now the hotel says the penthouse is not available. The President of the World Bank is here. With his entourage. Entourage! Yah... I met her last year in Gstaad.

(*Calls.*) V! Call to the Shah of Persia – the number is in the blue book – tell him I need a small favour.

We'll leak a little Persian oil, give the World Bank a fright.

Hotels! Horror stories, more like. Airlines all the same logo – 'Luggage to follow'. Can you believe where was my big trunk last week? Kuala Lumpur. 'Oh, Miss Dietrich, your lovely dresses!' Lovely dresses! (*Shakes her head.*) Uch-uch. You know what's inside? Electrical adaptors. When you are touring as long as me you don't take chances. Yah... agents, managers... fog, strike, crisis – "Take the Concorde, be here yesterday"... in the end, your work, the thing you dedicated your life to, denied yourself, lost friends for... the work – that becomes remote... immaterial. Only real thing is this mindless, endless, toxic voyage in space. You know what I am in the end – a long-distance truck driver.

So different from the old days. Hollywood... nineteen thirty. City of dreams for the whole world. And you know – it was just a sleepy little village, on the edge of nowhere. But so beautiful... to look out at the Pacific, always shining, orange groves right down to the sea – Oh and the air! Like Beaumes de Venise! Ultimate accolade. To be summoned to Hollywood. I never forget that first sea voyage. How to travel! Fine staterooms, orchestras, champagne, wonderful food out of this world, and every passenger on board talented, beautiful... everyone exciting.

I remember one day on deck this American woman –
so lovely, the face, the neck – dark hair, blue eyes,
like the Irish. The third night, after the cabaret, we are
standing by the rail, and so I kiss the neck. Why not?
My God! The scandal!

SONG: 'YOU DO SOMETHING TO ME'.

She was lovely. A bit like Greta Garbo only – you know
– good looking.

Grrreta Garrrbo. Always on the screen like she is
suffering some female problem down below. How can
you be so blue all the time? Well, yoghurt and mung
beans, what do you expect?

The phone rings.

(*Bawls.*) V! Get it, I don't take calls in the dressing room.

VIVIAN picks up the phone on the dressing table.

VIVIAN: De la part de qui? Hullo...?
Hullo... what?... listen, I can't hear you, is it an emer-
gency?

This woman is yelling so much I can't hear what
she's saying – calm down! Now she's crying.

MARLENE: (*Calmly.*) Don't worry, it's my girlfriend from
Palm Springs. Say I'm in traction, I'll call back.

VIVIAN speaks briefly into the phone and goes.

MARLENE: This is the woman who trades husbands for a
living – you know the sort... all widow's peak and no
lips – how does she do it? He's giving her half Palm
Springs and twenty million dollars and she's crying! You know why? Because she didn't get the dog.
Listen – with twenty million dollars she can afford
Lassie.

This is the woman, she gives a quarter to a blind man
she asks for change. Husband number six already lined

up... how? These days she looks like Joan Crawford after two hours of root canal. A lifetime of marriages? Not for me. I'd rather sell pumpernickel.

(Sings.) 'LOOK ME OVER CLOSELY'.

VIVIAN and MUTTI manhandle on a huge, hideously decorated artificial tree.

MARLENE: What on earth – ?

VIVIAN hands MARLENE the greetings card.

MARLENE: (*Reads.*) 'From the Management – with all our deepest love and admiration and good wishes for tonight's performance.' My God.

VIVIAN: 'The Thing from Outer Space?'

MARLENE: Sabotage, more like. (*Prowls round the thing.*) I can't even sell it.

VIVIAN: Sell it!

MARLENE: Take it away. Give it to Pierre on the door, he can throw it in the street.

VIVIAN: 'Offence will be taken.'

MARLENE: Say I have an allergy. Tell them to give it to Billy Graham when he arrives... or Liberace, the week after, he's into sparkle. Say instead I need more light in the wings and in here disinfectant and air freshener!

VIVIAN: (*Sing song.*) Your wish is my command.

VIVIAN and MUTTI manhandle the thing off.

MARLENE: (*Reminiscent.*) The things people send. Red silk camiknickers hand-embroidered with dirty message... a model of the Vatican in passe-partout, MARLENE around the dome, one E missing... flattened chocolates – tinned fruit! – once even a life-size portrait of me in the nude made of matchsticks from the St Quentin male voice choir.

Sometimes of course...

A lawn handkerchief with fine, fine embroidery from a woman in prison. She had killed her child. Photographs from the soldier who'd been with my father in that first terrible war. Pale kid gloves for ten years from a guy who never signed his full name. Then nothing. Did he die? Find another love? And the letter from the man in Chicago who wrote of his years in the stockyards. Together with a box made of mother of pearl which had belonged to his mother... not bad. He said that his life had been nothing. Not worth it. Except for the movies. And the movies he liked best were mine. He found me glamorous.

She sits up and sees her face in the glass.

OK, OK, we get to work.

MARLENE begins to unpack her boxes. She crosses calling for VIVIAN.

MARLENE: Baby, get me a beer... Heiney... no Kronenbourg – and some pretzels.

VIVIAN: Tout de suite.

VIVIAN looks in, waves cheerful assent and disappears. MARLENE unpacks her make-up onto her dressing table. She begins to go over the words of the song 'ILLUSIONS'. She half hums, sings a few lines, murmuring to herself. Notices MUTTI, who has fallen asleep.

MARLENE: (*Irritable.*) Oh, you took the wrong pills again! (*She sings, reprises, stops in some distress.*) My God, I remember nothing.

The words, some of these words I just don't have at all!

Mon Dieu! I can't go on tonight... impossible.

Agitated, she walks about. She spins, indecisive, then crosses behind the screen. She emerges with her medicine chest and searches among the bottles, muttering to herself. Finding the right tablets she tips two onto her palm and crosses to the dressing table. There she pours a glass of water. She makes to take the tablets then, changing her mind, puts down the glass of water.

MARLENE: No. (*She puts the tablets back into the bottle.*)

OK. We take you, we don't get the shakes.

But no shakes – no performance.

But she wavers, picks up the bottle again. And puts it down firmly.

No!

Nein, nein, nein!

'But Marlene.. all the great violinists take tranks...'

So we don't get any more Jascha Heifetz. Yah, I see why.

Nein.

I am the icon who does not fuck up.

You are Marlene... Marlene.

Pay the dues, sweetheart...

But she crosses urgently to the drinks table, pours herself a stiff whisky, drinks it fast, taking deep breaths.

MARLENE: (*Softly.*) I can't do it. Not tonight. Maybe to-morrow. No, no... oh no, no, no please...

She falls to her knees at MUTTI'S feet. MUTTI, waking, strokes her gently.

MARLENE: Watch the door. Don't let them see me like this. (*She looks up into MUTTI's face.*) Berlin, remember? That awful tour when they –

MUTTI kisses the top of MARLENE's head.

You were the only one who understood. About fear you knew everything. Oh my dear...

MUTTI strokes her gently. MARLENE begins to relax. VIVIAN enters, cheerfully noisy, with a tray.

VIVIAN: Pretzels and beer coming up!

MARLENE staggers to her feet, shaken and furious.

MARLENE: How dare you come in here without knocking! No-one is allowed to do that – not even the President!

VIVIAN, flustered, wheels, looking for a place for the tray.

VIVIAN: I'm sorry – I didn't realise I was intruding. (*She proffers the tray.*)

MARLENE: Take it away – I don't want it... Out! (*As VIVIAN, bewildered, finds a place in the background for the tray.*) Is it not enough that I have to clean my own dressing room, sit where everything I touch smells of old, wet dog... (*Wiping her hand over a surface.*) ... Ugh!!

VIVIAN: I'm sorry, I'm sorry.

MARLENE throws things around. VIVIAN follows, picking up. MUTTI escapes.

MARLENE: Filthy damn dressing room... dirty stage... not enough light in the wings so you take a fall just before your entrance... tell them now – more light!... and in the corridor carpet, all the way to the stage – now – before the half or I don't go on!

VIVIAN: I'll try.

MARLENE: No – not try! Do it!

VIVIAN: All right! Whatever you say!

MARLENE: Yah, whatever I say!

She waves VIVIAN off imperiously, and paces, furious.

MARLENE: They think you don't know... that you can't work it out... cheapskates! They think you didn't go... you weren't been... you wasn't... you was never there... down there with the rest, looking up.

Listen... don't begrudge us the best table, the penthouse. We pay for it. Glamour? It's in your heads, sweethearts, not ours. We are making it for you! Don't believe this wonderful smile in the photograph –

But no.

We must be put up high to knock down. Doesn't matter how generous you are – you think they love you, the little people? Hah!

'Here she comes, the Star!'

'You haven't seen her without wig and make-up – not so glamorous then, believe me. Here she comes – Trouble. Nothing is right for her.'

'We are treated like servants!'

Well that is what they are! Only they don't have the respect to do the job properly and get joy from it, but of course most of them are just filling in... 'Oh, but Miss Dietrich, I am no mere seamstress, I am really a designer...' How many designers do we need for God's sake? A seamstress now, used to be a good one on every corner, copy you a Chanel in two days... shoemakers too. Now everybody wants to play the heroine. Listen, half the time the heroine is Camille, and she doesn't finish so good.

SONG: 'ILLUSIONS'.

VIVIAN: (*Enters.*) The queue for returns is right round the block and as far as the Place! [*French pronunciation.*]

Daunted by MARLENE's lack of response, VIVIAN sprays perfume.

MARLENE: Ugh! What's that?

VIVIAN: You wanted air freshener.

MARLENE: But not the tomb of King Farouk!

VIVIAN: It's Fracas, you like it!

The phone rings. VIVIAN answers.

VIVIAN: Vivian Hoffman... hold the line. (*She holds out the phone to MARLENE.*) The *New York Times.*

MARLENE: (*Shakes her head violently.*) What do they want?

VIVIAN: It's your interview.

MARLENE: Interview?

VIVIAN: Your interview with the *New York Times.*

MARLENE: I don't want to talk to them, you deal with it. Deal with it!

VIVIAN: (*To the phone.*) I'm sorry, we're paging Miss Dietrich now, I'll see if she is... Sunday?

MARLENE: What?

VIVIAN: You're playing Carnegie for charity next week, remember?

MARLENE: Carnegie, Schmarnegie.

VIVIAN: (*Into the phone.*) A whole page?

MARLENE: (*In a marked manner.*) No – interview.

VIVIAN: The front page?

MARLENE: They can go to hell, tell them to go to hell.

VIVIAN: And a photo session?

MARLENE: Photo session?

VIVIAN: Two pages? I'm afraid I can't confirm, I don't know if Miss Dietrich is available –

MARLENE: V, for God's sake, what are you saying?

VIVIAN: And you're here now?

MARLENE: Where?

VIVIAN: Hold the line. They're at the *George V.*

MARLENE: Just around the corner?

VIVIAN: With a photographer.

MARLENE: What? Who? What is going on?

VIVIAN: The photographer is Arnie.

MARLENE: (*Pleased.*) Arnie? Arnie?

VIVIAN: Yuh, and she'll do stills and, if you want, eight by sixes for mailout.

MARLENE: For free?

VIVIAN nods.

OK. The interview today – ten minutes, and the photo session in the morning, three hours.

VIVIAN: Ten minutes? For the award winning Stafford McCloud?

MARLENE: OK, quarter of an hour.

VIVIAN: Hullo? Miss Dietrich will see you. We'll try to fit you in. I'll meet you in the foyer. I'll tell her, thank you very much. (*Replaces phone.*) He says salootay... he can't wait to say hullo, and he'll definitely get you a double page spread, with full front page pic.

MARLENE: Good. (*Sings.*) 'Want to buy some illusions, slightly used, second hand...'

VIVIAN is delving into a large wooden box.

MARLENE: Oh, my photos.

She rises looking around her, deciding.

MARLENE: Let's see, Eisenhower on the top and Church-ill underneath. And De Gaulle, what do we do with De Gaulle now we're in Paris? OK – a special place for him on the table. You know I have medals from all three of these guys and yet I never did it with a single one of them, how about that?

VIVIAN: Medals for good behaviour?

MARLENE laughs.

MARLENE: Impressive, huh? Well, you know... Eisen-hower was a country boy, little bit shy. Churchill? Too old – would have been risky, he was too valuable to lose... after all, I am a patriot.

VIVIAN: Of course. What about De Gaulle?

MARLENE: De Gaulle? Ahh... the General. (*Sings.*) 'It's not that he couldn't... It's not that he wouldn't... '

VIVIAN laughs.

VIVIAN: So. What kept you?

MARLENE: Never the right moment. But a friskier man than you think – stood very close to me on the parade. (*Leaning suggestively into VIVIAN.*) Oh, you're losing a button, I'll fix it for you.

She takes needle and cotton, deftly sews on VIVIAN's cuff button, leaning by her side. Looks up.

MARLENE: When do you open?

VIVIAN: September. Boston, Philly – with good luck, Broadway. I may need to rework Act Two – we'll do a little workshop in the Catskills.

MARLENE: When?

VIVIAN: May.

MARLENE: I think I'm free!

VIVIAN: If you come no-one will look at the actors.

MARLENE: I'll wear a wig, like in *Witness for the Prosecution*.

VIVIAN: Well *then* they'll ALL know you. (*She sighs.*) Can you make the fall?

MARLENE: The premiere? Why not?

VIVIAN: It would help!

MARLENE: What's wrong?

VIVIAN: A change of style. You'll get it, thousands won't.

MARLENE: Be brave. Beat them over the head.

VIVIAN laughs.

Insist! "Trust the artist!"

VIVIAN: Artist?! Marlene, you can't call yourself that these days, they kill you for it. (*Flat.*) For the only thing you have.

MARLENE: So protect yourself! Listen, if you wished only for peace and quiet you should have stayed with the little lectures on Proust.

VIVIAN: Maybe I should. (*She holds out the last picture.*) Where do you want Hemingway?

MARLENE: To be a writer...

They stand, heads together, looking at the photograph of Ernest Hemingway. Then VIVIAN gives a wry grin, puts her hands briefly on MARLENE's shoulders, kisses her on the cheek and goes out quickly. MARLENE watches her for an instant and then looks at the photograph once more, tracing the lines of Hemingway's face with her finger.

MARLENE: Oh baby – I was so proud to be your friend.

Ernest Hemingway, the great American tough guy.

Only we know different, don't we sweetheart?

She sat on your shoulders all right – the Black Empress.

Fools!

Did they really believe that you were just a big hunk? That to be only butch would make it possible for you to write *A Farewell to Arms*?

I know you suffered, baby. (*She almost breaks down.*) But did you have to shoot yourself? Destroy that beautiful head?

(*She recovers.*) We had some good times, eh? Remember Paris? Walking down the Champs Élysées with that damn gun under your belly to relieve the Ritz Hotel?

Great days, Papa.

In the end you couldn't be in the same room with him.

I loved him like a child – a father – a brother – lover too.

We got old, Papa.

Shouldn't happen.

Song: 'I WISH YOU LOVE'.

VIVIAN, entering upstage, steps back discreetly to listen. At the end of the song MARLENE, seeing VIVIAN in the shadow, jumps, startled, and is furious.

MARLENE: Knock why don't you? How can I be alone when people are in and out all the time like it was Grand Central Station! I have a performance to do!

VIVIAN: Marlene, I'm sorry... (*Going.*)

MARLENE: Where are you going, get back here!

VIVIAN: What?

MARLENE: (*Agitated.*) I don't have my hot flannels – where are my hot flannels... and the beer, did you get the beer? (*As VIVIAN swoops forward with the tray.*)

– I don't want it now, take it away – where is Billy, I have a song to go through, some of these words I don't have at all, I need the sheets – (*As VIVIAN dashes off to get them.*) – where is everybody, what are they doing? Music... come on... I need some action!

My trouble is I'm too Nice with everyone! (*She slams out of the door, going offstage.*)

(*Offstage.*) The songsheets, where are they? For God's sakes! What are they all doing, find the Stage Manager – who are you, get him out – Out! V! Did you find the dots? The sheets! No, no, no!! These are all in the wrong Key! What is that and who put it there – looks like a funeral wreath, take it away, I'm not dead yet – send it to Betty Davis... out, out!

VIVIAN runs frantically into the dressing room.

VIVIAN: (*Panicking.*) Beer, flannels, flowers... Oh God! (*Mutters.*) Music, music, music!... (*She forages desperately, finds the right sheets, dashes offstage.*)

MARLENE: (*Offstage.*) There is no carpet – why? No carpet, no show... tell them! V? Mutti – where is Mutti?

MARLENE enters fast, VIVIAN running after her with the songsheets.

Ah! My music! At last – sweetheart, are you all right, you look peaky. (*Alarmed.*) You don't have a virus – you're not getting sick?

VIVIAN: (*Faintly.*) No. (*Shakes her head.*) Absolutely not. I'm just –

MARLENE: Good. Take a rest while I go through this.

VIVIAN exits, exhausted.

(*Calls.*) Billy, I'm all yours!

MARLENE walks onto the empty stage. She takes off her jacket, nods to the PIANIST.

MARLENE begins to sing 'LOLA'. And stops. She looks upwards and around at the lights.

MARLENE: Wait a minute. What's happening with the lights here... here, down here. This is dreadful, so dark, we're not doing *Night Train to Munich*, you know – this is a very important spot, here I do my bows – you have it completely dark and horrible. (*Light change but MARLENE is not satisfied.*)

(*Calls up to LIGHTING MAN.*) Could we have a little thirty-six? Even better – Surprise Pink? Yah?

Light change.

Ahh! That's much better. Thank you! Now we're cooking with gas.

She sings some more, then looks up again.

MARLENE: (*Calls.*) Now I'm Tight Iris, yah?

Lights focus on her. She nods, sings some more, moving about the stage. Stops dead.

MARLENE: Oh now please – this is Horrible! Total dark! Here is most important spot for me... I pick up the flowers, maybe touch the hands, why bother if they can't see me – look, more light here – please!

(*Stands, tapping her foot.*) Is anyone listening to me up there?

More Light!!

The stage is flooded with light. Gratified, MARLENE finishes the song.

MARLENE: OK. Take five. Billy, Edie's feeling better? – good. Remind her... stay off solid fats. She should take just a little olive oil, then the joints are improved.

Crosses, going upstage for a large broom, muttering to herself.

MARLENE: (*Muttering.*) Such filth you wouldn't believe – they are paid to clean and who cleans? I clean. Should be ashamed... what is the matter with them? The world is full of people who don't do what you pay them for...

She takes the broom and starts to sweep the stage with rhythmic, competent sweeps. She hums, murmuring words to herself from time to time. The sweeping seems to relax her. She tries a few dance steps, her mood lightening.

And then her leg gives way and she falls.

MARLENE: Oh – my leg!...

MUTTI, upstage, hovers, anxious.

(*She tries to rise.*) No... please, not now... (*She tries to rise.*) Oh God, I can't get up. (*She gasps in pain, calls out.*) Verdammt leg... You made it too tight!

MUTTI comes down to her. She bends, to attend to MARLENE. Who waves her off.

MARLENE: No, no... later... help me up, for God's sakes, before they see me... ahhh!

She gasps in pain as MUTTI, with difficulty, helps her onto her feet and offstage.

Fade to black.

End of Act One.

ACT TWO

MARLENE and VIVIAN enter from the back of the stage.

MARLENE: What time is it?

VIVIAN: You just asked me that.

MARLENE: The time!

VIVIAN: (*Looks at her watch.*) Nearly four. (*As MARLENE stumbles slightly.*) Are you all right, Marlene?

MARLENE: Of course I am all right. Where are they, why aren't they here?

VIVIAN: (*Calls to auditorium.*) Are the usherettes ready – oh, they're coming – here, your notebook with their names and birthdays.

MARLENE: Ah – Yvette I know... Marie Séverine... Elise, Jolie, Katya, Marie-Claire. Right – now you know what to do on curtain down?

VIVIAN: I do.

MARLENE: No-one – no-one is allowed to tread on the stage.

VIVIAN: Absolutely.

MARLENE: You'll be in the wings with the little bag for the sequins?

VIVIAN: And you'd like me to sweep the stage?

MARLENE: No!! *I* sweep the stage. If I don't do it myself you bet every sequin, every little bead that falls off the dress doesn't get picked up for me to sew back on. Just be there.

VIVIAN: Understood. (*Hisses.*) They're here... the usherettes...

MARLENE: Hullo girls. Nice to see you again! Thank you... I'm always so pleased to be back. What happened to Yvette? Oh, I'm sorry to hear that. Now... I need three of you. (*She points.*) Name? Elise... and... ah, Marie Séverine, ah you have a birthday tomorrow... you see, I remember... and... Katya. Thank you so much... (*Waves the others away.*) Maybe the younger ones next time.

Come closer, yah? (*She gestures for them to gather close.*)

Now. This we do every night.

VIVIAN: Tonight... and every night.

MARLENE: Yah, every night. This is Miss Hoffman who is assisting me... she will give you flowers at the back of the stalls while I am doing the last number. Please be sure to be prompt and in your places. Then... start to bring the flowers, very slow, when I am making my first exit – be halfway down when I return.

VIVIAN: When Miss Dietrich is halfway to the footlights.

MARLENE: Yah, that's right... thank you Vivian. And all the time look up at me... smiling... hold up the flowers high, but I won't see them, then I look down – oh... no, not for me... oh!... so beautiful... and Elise, chérie, you are ready with the next bouquet, and I don't see you either and I go... oh... so kind... and I see Katya, and Katya I kiss – no! Wait a minute... who is the oldest... Elise, you are seventy? Marvellous... You I kiss!

Now don't worry, just hold the flowers high and keep smiling and looking into my eyes, you'll all be wonderful. Thank you girls, I'll see you later, don't worry about a thing!

She bends, kisses her fingers, waves them away solicitously.

MARLENE: (*To VIVIAN, brisk.*) Make sure the flowers go

straight into water backstage, they have to last the whole week, and don't forget the roses for the boys to throw down from the dressing room windows when I do the autographs.

VIVIAN: At the stage door?

MARLENE: Yah, Victor will be at the performance tonight and after the show he will lift me onto the roof of the car and I'll wave, and they will throw down the flowers and it will all be very nice and Victor will hand me the programmes to sign so I won't need to bend over so much. Ouf! (*Of tiredness.*)

VIVIAN: Marlene, you're tired. You're doing too much. Why not cut the stage door routine tonight, we'll slip you out front of house.

MARLENE: (*Puzzled.*) Front of house? Are you mad? Now. Victor will tell the driver when to move off – he must drive very slowly through the fans, make sure he is told, so that I can touch the hands and wave. Then when the crowd thins out – I will judge this – he must go very fast – tell him that too. We arrive to the hotel, I do more autographs, photographs, more flowers, then you will say I must go upstairs, Miss Dietrich is tired, she must now rest. The manager escorts me to the elevator, we go up to the suite, he kisses my hand, I thank him, you thank him, I go in, you close the door, and then, only then, the performance is over.

VIVIAN: Got it. (*Shakes her head in admiration.*)

MARLENE kisses her on the cheek.

MARLENE: Poor baby. Tough, uh?

VIVIAN: Not a bit.

MARLENE: Hah. Don't tell me you didn't think of ringing the airline more than once.

VIVIAN: Not once.

MARLENE: Oh? I'm surprised.

VIVIAN: You shouldn't be.

MARLENE: Why not, I give you a bad time. You don't
need to stay, you don't need me.

VIVIAN: You know why I stay.

MARLENE: Do I?

VIVIAN: Of course you do. I love you.

MARLENE: Oh – that.

VIVIAN: Yes – that.

MARLENE: You and the world, baby. No – I don't mean
it, I'm glad you came.

*VIVIAN gives her a tisane in a glass. She sips, lies back in
the chair.*

VIVIAN: Close your eyes.

VIVIAN massages MARLENE's neck.

Slight pause.

VIVIAN: Marlene?

MARLENE: Yah?

VIVIAN: Let me stay.

MARLENE: What about your work?

VIVIAN: I don't care about the work.

MARLENE: Yes you do.

VIVIAN: Please.

MARLENE: No, darling.

What does Billy mean – 'new songs'? I don't do new,
I do old!

VIVIAN sighs.

MARLENE: Always they say do this, do that... and when you say no – bad atmosphere. Who has to go out there? Me! Alone! I make all the arrangements, I pay all the bills...

VIVIAN: Don't upset yourself.

MARLENE: Do you know how brave you must be to do this? You don't do it without courage, believe me. I am a Viking.

VIVIAN: You are, darling, you are.

MARLENE: Don't be mean with the audience, he says. I am never mean... I am generous – always!

VIVIAN: Mostly.

MARLENE: What do you mean, mostly? I always say yes.

VIVIAN: (*Laughs.*) We know that!

MARLENE: Why not? Only takes a minute. (*She laughs.*) Then they can say – Marlene? Oh I had her. Marlene Dietrich? I know her *very* well. Better to share it out, huh? – creates a better climate. Little smile across the room, wave of the hand... people have good memories, they are nicer, more open-handed.

VIVIAN: Use it, you mean?

MARLENE: You bet! I ask all the time favours from loving slaves... here, give me a nice kiss...

They kiss.

That is to be practical, what is life if not that? Anyway, my mother always told me it was rude to say no.

MARLENE crosses behind the screen. VIVIAN, blue, takes a drink.

MARLENE: I think I fire Billy. You can't change things! Change the songs?

He must be mad! I am like the Sam Browne belt
– created for a purpose! 'Don't change anything' they
say to me at the stage door. I make them think... I make
them believe they won't die after all. Look, here she
is again – oh, so lovely... glamorous... the wonderful
cheekbones, the fabulous dress, the white fur, the
blonde, blonde hair... and all the same *songs*.

(*Emerging from behind screen in an elegant dressing gown.
She sings a line from 'MEIN BLONDES BABY'.*) 'That
one sends me back Miss Dietrich.' (*She sings a line from
'LIEBE OHNE LIEBE'.*) 'That one always make me
cry!' Yah. It's what I'm for. You want gemütlich... get a
Hun.

(*Sits.*) Anyway... When the camera doesn't love you
anymore, how do you make the rest of your life? What
to do? Become the famous recluse? Appear in bad
horror movies? Go for the quiet life?

(*She looks at VIVIAN with a grin.*) Plenty of time for that
in the cemetery, eh? No. Anyway, how is it possible to
survive without it?

VIVIAN: Without what? Sex?

MARLENE: Sex... no, no... That I never really cared for
so much... no, no, no – the oxygen!

VIVIAN: Oxygen?

MARLENE: To have it turned off, like a faucet, like a tap.

VIVIAN: Oh, you mean – ?

MARLENE: The worship! The adoration. Listen, I have
no pity for the poor little movie star that ruined her
private life, spent all her money and now... quelle
pitié... She is not bankable anymore. Happens to us
all, baby.

When you are fifteen... seventeen... even nineteen... you are an empress. You reign! The world picks up the tab. 'Girls allowed in free.' Boys too.

But when you are not eighteen and you want to stay in that world... what then?

You bite the bullet and you pay the price mein Herr.

You know, in thirty years I never ate a meal where I didn't get up from the table hungry. And food is important to me, I love to cook. Many men in my bedroom – very few in my kitchen.

I have this dream – comes again and again. A chalet in the mountains... Spring... the snow has melted. I am sitting at a table on the verandah, comes the proprietor with a silver dish... big... and behind him his wife with new bread and a pile of fresh butter... and he has this ham, still glistening from the pot, and the wife mit the dumplings, and he begins to carve this fine meat... all crumbling away from the knife, with pink juices... I lift my fork...

And I wake up.

If you want it baby, you pay the price. Maybe Lana Turner was discovered at the counter of Schwabb's Drugstore, we all dream of the lucky break... but luck, oh luck comes to those who work for it. Energy! We all have it. How to use it right! Not waste all in envy... in fantasy, blaming... 'I am the middle child... I was not loved?' Love yourself! Why do you think the good Lord invented masturbation?

VIVIAN: Touchée.

They laugh.

MARLENE: No. You got to be tough. Do it by yourself – for yourself, or the talent is wasted.

VIVIAN kisses MARLENE on the cheek.

VIVIAN: Not your talent.

MARLENE: Me?! I never had a talent!
Listen! Why did... why... why am I a movie star?

VIVIAN shrugs, not knowing the required answer.

MARLENE: Because Jo Sternberg, as the Americans so
charmingly put it, wanted to get into my drawers.

Dear Jo. Now there was talent if you like. Such lighting.
Everything I know about lighting, and I know a lot, I
learnt from Jo. Crazy for me. Like Selznick for Jennifer
Jones. Jennifer Jones the lady with two expressions...

"My God, I think I'm pregnant. Thank God, the test was
negative."

You think Jane Russell could act? Rita? Mind you,
doesn't always work. Zanuck broke his ass trying to
make Juliette Greco a star.

VIVIAN: Who?

MARLENE: Exactly. No, for the movies, must be something else. The love affair. With the camera. If you
are loved by the camera you are a star. Doesn't matter stupid story, silly frocks. People remember the
moment.

'Remember when she rode the horse up the steps of
the palace?'

'Remember the fight with Una Merkel?'

'Remember when she walked in the desert in high
heels? When she leaned out of the train, with the smoke
and the veil...?'

If the camera is for you... if you are loved by the
camera – that's it. Gary Cooper?... opened his mouth
only when he had to, believe me. Who cared? The
man was beautiful and the camera told us everything.
Of course you have to know what you are doing.

The phone rings, she grimaces at VIVIAN to answer it.

VIVIAN: Vivian Hoffman. Oui, d'accord.

She puts the phone down.

VIVIAN: It's your interview.

MARLENE: Interview... what interview?

VIVIAN: With the *New York Times*. He's waiting for you in the auditorium.

MARLENE rises, pushing VIVIAN aside.

MARLENE: Why didn't you tell me? My God it's too late, I have a show to do! Mutti?... Where is that bitch woman, never there when she is wanted –

VIVIAN: I – ah – I think she's feeling ill. (*Gestures frantically behind MARLENE's back to MUTTI, who creeps away to hide.*)

MARLENE: This time she is fired... (*Going off.*)

VIVIAN exits. Short pause.

MARLENE appears, looking glamorous, for her interview with Stafford McCloud.

MARLENE: (*Smoky.*) Hullo.

This interview – it will be syndicated?

Coast to coast? And abroad? Where abroad?

Placated she nods regally, sits, crossing her legs seductively. Leans down to the auditorium.

Naturally I see the copy before you release it?

General Eisenhower always accorded me that courtesy when I was in the battle zones during the war. I don't see it, they don't read it... you take your choice.

Yah, I'm sure we make an agreeable compromise.
I would never censor, I am for a free world. Within
reason.

Oh, you have a list of questions? Good, we don't waste
time. (*Leans forward, listens.*)

Why do I tour? Because I can't disappoint my beloved
audiences! Not at all, I love the work. I adore to travel.
Wonderful airlines to look after you... hotels... (*Double-
edged.*) I am so grateful to the hotels of this world for
their... (*Searches for a word.*) ... (*Treble-edged.*) ... wonderful
courtesy and efficiency.

Of course I am married, didn't you do your homework?
(*She leans forward to listen.*) So he lives in another
country, what's the difference? Next question. And
don't forget to mention my beautiful daughter.

Out... out! (*This to VIVIAN who has crept in behind her with
flowers. She moves to the interviewer.*)

More flowers!... oh... they are from you... (*She takes them
from VIVIAN, buries her nose in them briefly.*)

So delicious... dahlias. (*Thrusts them back at VIVIAN,
waves her off.*) Religion? We-ell, I never had any
problem with God, he has always been most
charming with me. (*Sips her drink.*)

Holidays? Uch-uch. When I am free I see my family,
friends... I don't backpack, believe me. I don't say I
wouldn't... why not, if it's not fattening?

Of course I like music... (*She rolls her eyes with boredom.*) I
am a German! Not Mahler. Because he is like a bowl of
coffee ice cream only the waiter was too slow.

Sure I like jazz. The women are the best, the women
you believe... Bessie Smith, Billie Holliday... Edith.

Yes, I knew Piaf. We were very close.

(*Pause.*) In the end I abandoned her.

(*She shrugs.*) She was impossible. On the stage though, incomparable. There she is the Empress and I am the slave with the jar on the head.

No, don't say I have a great voice.

Because it's not true.

You seek to flatter with a lie... you think the artist needs this? All art is truth, even the little art which I am trying to do has its own truth. I said to James Mason once when he came round after a show... 'So Jimmy, what do you think of the voice?' He says 'It's divine, you have a marvellous voice' – I threw him out! Next question.

Too boring, next.

Orson? What can I say? Orson Welles is a genius – a titan. (*Leans forward.*) For no-one else would I have played the madame of a Mexican whorehouse. For Orson I would do it for nothing – well I did. Wonderful to work with – so intelligent. Tell me... how can he be so intelligent and so fat?

I wouldn't know what makes a good husband. A star can't have husbands.

Well I do have a husband – but I knew him before I was famous so it's OK. When you are a star – well – fine at first when he wants to do it with you all the time, but after that... (*She pulls a face.*)

You really want to know?

Off the record? OK. First, familiarity going nasty – clothes on the floor, bits of food left in the basin when they do their teeth, the John left unflushed. Then the memory loss... 'You didn't get the message from your mother... the studio? So sorry.' Then the small infidelities... with the maid, the stand-in... no, not usually the stand-in, too close to home. Then you go to sign the cheque for tax... oh la la, the till is empty. 'But Monsieur said you were not to be disturbed – this is not your signature?' Last of all the greatest betrayal. 'She is younger than you. She is more beautiful. She is bigger at the box office.'

PA announcement: 'Miss Dietrich your half-hour call please, gentlemen of the band your half-hour call. Thank you.'

MARLENE: I'm so sorry. You have enough? Thank you, not at all, you are very sweet... so long as you don't tell me I got a great voice.

On the contrary I sound like a duck shoot on a salt marsh in Siberia. Why do you think I wear the dress? So they forget the voice! (*She laughs.*)

Oh... you have a nice laugh. Tell me, are you moody?

Nothing. I like a moody man, that's all.

Give my love to your beautiful city. And don't believe everything you write about me.

Song: 'JONNY'.

VIVIAN: (*Enters, excited.*) Marlene, the house is open – it's packed out already! Le tout Paris – they can't wait!

MARLENE: I'm not going on.

VIVIAN: What?

MARLENE: I can't do it.

VIVIAN: Darling – (*Hugs MARLENE.*) of course you can, of course you can!

MARLENE nods. Reassured, VIVIAN goes.

MARLENE: (*Alone, she shakes her head.*) I can't.

How do you know?

How do you know you can do it this time? Maybe this is the day you can't go out there any more... this is the day it finishes.

You should take something! Everybody does... Von Karajan... Larry Olivier... Cary Grant! What you are feeling is natural, the doctor said so, the specialist... your reactions are normal. Normal reaction to stressful situation.

It's OK!

Take the tranks!

Why must you all the time be the Junker's daughter? The Hun who came in from the cold.

The good German.

She moves, tries her legs. And lifts the skirts of her dressing gown. And we see that one of her legs is bandaged.

MARLENE: That damn woman!... it's too tight... it's cutting me off, I'm not going to get onstage... oh my God... another night of the long knives...

If I take painkillers then the speech is blurred and I can't see and we have another little fall.

She sits, disconsolate. She lays her head back and closes her eyes.

MARLENE: (*Murmurs.*) What am I doing here?

I could be lying by the beach, seeing old friends, listening to music.

Where I should be is with the daughter. She needs me. I should be with the grandchildren, doing what grandmothers do, and I'm good at it. I'm missing the best, those years so quick of their childhood and I'm not there. Do we know how long we got? I can't afford to miss one beautiful day!

It's My turn to sit in the corner. Why don't I settle for the
verandah and lift the face to the sun and smell the stocks
and the tobacco flowers...what am I trying to prove?
I already proved it! My life is on film, in cans, on reels...
I am forever the Scarlet Empress... the verdammt Blue
Angel! How many people have their lives patchworked
into dream and fantasy and preserved like the best
Black Forest fruit of the berry jam. In a hundred... a
thousand years... I can still be! Marlene for ever.

Who cares?

I am an old woman. Why don't I seek the truth of that...
celebrate that... be in the centre of who I am, where I
am, what I am?

And what are you, Marie-Magdalene – Marlene?

Who are you? Who?

After the first war – possible.

Honour.

They lost so many. We lost so many.

Cut down. Both sides.

But the next war......

(*Pause.*) I was not there! I left in 1930, to be a movie star.
I left for the money and for fame, and because
Jo says I must, so we leave.

I didn't go back.

My work was in America.

And then, in Germany...

In Germany it was not good. If you were Jewish, not
good at all. Or socialist. Or gipsy, or homosexual.
Would I have left, for that reason... for reasons of

prudence and because of fear and loathing, and refusal to join?

I think so.

Oh yes.

After Krystallnacht for sure.

You don't burn books. Only devils do things with fire.

Goebbels wanted me back, to lead his film industry. I said no. Many times.

I am an American citizen.

With my German accent.

(*Pause.*) You are German, Marie-Magdalene – Marlene.

Your home is Germany.

I am in exile.

Pause. She groans quietly, shifts, easing her legs.

Ex-patriate. An exiled person.

In time.

In space.

I am in severe exile.

She sits upright suddenly.

You want to take the blame. Even if you were not there you want to take the blame, even if you did not know!

Or if you did not know enough... if you knew too little.

If you chose to know too little.

Then. There.

At the time.

Take the blame? Stupid.

What sort of gesture is that?

Hanh?!

What are you going to do – request to be flayed alive? Be tied like Prometheus to the rock?

What can be adequate?

What recompense?

She can only laugh at the thought.

The most civilised country – Beethoven, Brahms... the most civilised cruelty. With every modern refinement. Most – efficient.

Genocide.

My own country.

My people. (*Music for 'WARUM'.*)

The people of my flesh... of my mind... my uncles, my cousins... my forebears.

All implicated.

We did not know!

Don't believe it.

We knew.

MARLENE sings 'WARUM'.

MARLENE: When I went to Germany on the tour in fifty-one I had a good and brave heart inside. Don't go, they said, but I had to go. I had to tell that the forgiveness must begin, that I knew... who better, that there were good Germans, and here I am – a good German, and now it is all over, no more war, and we are ready to forgive, go forward.

And when I went back they spat on me for a traitor.

That's hard.

That's very hard. In your own home.

Home.

Yah. The place where you belong. Where you Feel...
you Know you belong... which actually you take for
granted.

Home. Where everything is familiar and so, everything
is as it should be. Habits coming naturally, not having
to be learned. No need to adapt... get the phrases right.
All there for you, absorbed as a baby, as a child. The
investment of your childhood. Your preparing days.

I need my own! My own village. The town along
the valley for a haircut... the city twice a year for
excitement, for the birthday.

I am an American.

Who... like every American... is not an American.

An exile.

And now it all begins again.

'Get out – this country was ours two thousand years ago,
give it back.'

'We have old scores to settle, sell us some arms!'

God, when will they ever learn?

*She lies back exhausted. Light change. A bell rings and VIVIAN
appears. MARLENE is alert at once.*

OK, sweetheart. Let's see if we can fool them one more
time. (*She goes followed by VIVIAN.*)

(*Offstage.*) Easy... take it very slowly...

VIVIAN: Breathe in.

MARLENE: I am breathing in!

Good... good.

Don't DO that!

Mutti!!

60

Introductory music.

MARLENE: (*Recorded.*) V, give me the glass... the hand glass! Now stand to one side... how does it look, does it look right?

VIVIAN: It looks fabulous. Turn round.

MARLENE: Then out of the way, how am I supposed to move?... all this toodle toodle toodle...

VIVIAN: You look sensational... wonderful...

PA: Mesdames et Messieurs... Ladies and Gentlemen... Ce moment que vous attendiez... The moment that you've all been waiting for... Mademoiselle... Marlene.. Dietrich!!!

Music.

MARLENE makes her entrance. She glides on in her tight, shimmering dress, trailing a swansdown coat. She traverses the stage twice, slips off the coat, throwing it off her shoulders with an imperious gesture and approaches the microphone. Applause. MARLENE stands, an icon, head bowed, absorbing the applause without acknowledgement. She lifts her head at last.

MARLENE sings 'THE LAZIEST GIRL IN TOWN'.

MARLENE: When I came first to America, after *The Blue Angel*, they told me 'Marlene, let us write for you tender love songs... songs for a siren to sing... sweet and low' and I said 'Sure'... and this, for one of my movies, is what they wrote for me.

MARLENE sings 'SEE WHAT THE BOYS IN THE BACK ROOM WILL HAVE'.

MARLENE sings 'MAKING WHOOPEE'.

MARLENE: This is a song very close to my heart. I sang it during the war. I sang it for three long years. I sang it through Africa, through Sicily, Italy – through Alaska, Iceland, Greenland, through England, Belgium, Holland... through Czechoslovakia, through France – and Germany. The soldiers loved it... Lili Marlene.

MARLENE sings 'LILI MARLENE'.

MARLENE removes her coat offstage.

MARLENE sings 'HONEYSUCKLE ROSE'.

MARLENE: It was my privilege, at the request of General Eisenhower, to visit the battle zones, during the war, to entertain the troops. On those long journeys I saw many things. I saw beautiful places destroyed. I saw women and children made hungry, homeless. And I saw young men, wounded, in hospital. I saw them die. I saw the waste of it all.

MARLENE sings 'WHERE HAVE ALL THE FLOWERS GONE?'

MARLENE sings 'LA VIE EN ROSE'.

MARLENE takes a call centre stage right. She receives flowers from the usherettes, stage right, takes another call stage centre, more flowers, receives flowers stage left, and leaves the stage.

MARLENE enters.

MARLENE: All right. This is the song from *The Blue Angel.* With my thanks – for your pleasure.

MARLENE sings 'FALLING IN LOVE AGAIN'.

The End.

OBEDIENTLY YOURS, ORSON WELLES

By Richard France

PREFACE

Orson Welles was rightfully contemptuous of academics, refusing all the honorary degrees that he was offered and heaping scorn on those of his 'learned "bee-ographers"' who dared to base our writings about his life and accomplishments on anything other than the charming fairy tales that he had so skillfully crafted over the years.

Frankly, it's hard to fault him on either count. These, after all, were the same fairy tales that sustained him long after the 'pigeons' (as he called potential investors) stopped returning his phone calls. And had he lived long enough to witness the birth of nanotechnology, there can be no doubt that he, too, would have recognized it as the only known substance on the face of this earth smaller than the mind of an academic.

I was living on a small farm in southern Maine at the time, annotating the third and final playscript – the enormous crazy quilt known as 'Five Kings' – for *Orson Welles on Shakespeare*, when I received an offer from the University of Southern California to spend a year as visiting associate professor with their (so-called) Theatre Division, now even more pretentiously known as its School of Theatre.

'Stay put,' I was told, especially by the very few academics whom I respected. 'That place is known on campus as USC's own little gulag.'

I'd been eking out a living by doing voice-overs in Boston, a two-hour drive from my home. And while debt-free, there were no windfalls awaiting me in Maine. So, the opportunity to triple my average income for a year, plus a $2,500 stipend to pay for the visuals and to index the *Welles on Shakespeare* book, plus a subsidized apartment above the smog line in Laurel Canyon proved irresistible. I was also able to convince myself that since we'd be parting company in such short order, even the vilest and most insecure of my colleagues would realise that I was no threat to them. Silly me!

Some years earlier, the Asian-American company, East West Players, had produced *Station J*, my epic about the evacuation and internment of our Japanese population during World War Two. So, when I alerted my good friend, Mako, that I'd be in Los Angeles, he invited me to return to East West as his dramaturg. In addition, a number of my voice-over clients in Boston apprised me of a recording studio in LA where, through a process known as phone-patching, we could continue working together.

Did I say *triple* my income? Mako introduced me to an LA agent, and I was soon recording promos and commercials for clients out there, as well.

From the outset, it was agreed to that none of these outside activities were to interfere with my primary responsibility, which was to my students. Even so, I soon found myself in the cross-hairs of a particularly venomous *assistant* professor.

'I don't see how Dr. France can continue doing everything he's doing', she hissed at one of our faculty meetings, prompting two of the deadest of the department's deadwood to bob their hollowed-out heads in agreement.

'Eventually, something has to suffer.'

'Such as?' I asked.

'We hope it won't be your classes, Richard,' the older, and even dumber, of the two deadwood chimed in.

My assurances that I would never allow that to happen, and it *never* did, seemed to put the matter at rest. Or so I imagined. In fact, the poison had only just begun to spread.

When the time came, and my student evaluations far surpassed my 'bitch noir,' she merely dismissed these results as 'gender distinction,' and intensified her campaign to discredit me.

Early in the second semester, I was in my office, with the door open, when one of my graduate students, an acting major from South Africa, appeared, crying hysterically. 'My mother!' she blurted out. 'She's dead!'

All I could think of was trying to comfort her as I guided her to a chair. We sat across from each other, holding hands, as she revealed what happened. Not only was her mother's death completely unexpected, by the time word of it reached my student it was too late for her to return to South Africa for the funeral.

The following week, I found myself in the provost's office, charged with sexually harassing the student whom I had simply tried to comfort. Also present was my dean, the very person who had persuaded me to spend that year at USC, looking even more sanctimonious than usual. 'What would you have done,' I asked him, making no attempt to disguise my anger, 'let her fall on the floor?' (He didn't know it at the time but his days at USC were also numbered.)

Confronting one's accuser is (supposedly) a cornerstone of American justice. It wasn't my student, that I was sure of. But when I asked who then (as if I couldn't guess), I was denied that information on the grounds that I might also get it into my head to harass my accuser. And given my angry reaction to the disgusting charges I was facing, both my dean and the provost considered this a real possibility.

The air of hypocrisy in that room was stultifying. The gospel of political correctness has utterly emasculated these two pitiful creatures. Since they lacked the decency to do so, I took it upon myself to identify my accuser, adding a word of warning: 'You guys better hope that sick cookie isn't eyeing your scalps, as well.'

Thereafter, every pretense of professional civility was replaced by the true and abiding ugliness of academic life. My (so-called) colleagues were instructed to limit their interaction with me to three syllables, 'good morning' or 'good evening', and only then if such an encounter was absolutely unavoidable – and I initiated it. I was also made *persona non grata* at that monumental waste-of-time known as faculty meetings, which my dean began holding at secret locations off-campus so that I, and another colleague he had turned on, could be excluded.

Personally, I was delighted. So too were my Boston clients, who offered to fill these extra hours away from USC with even more recording opportunities.

The sound studio in LA that they had directed me to also turned out to be where Welles had done so much of his final work as a voice-over performer – most notably, the dozen or so short stories that he had been commissioned to read (in English) by a Japanese entrepreneur, who then marketed them to school children in his country as a teaching tool. Welles and his little dog, Kiki, would be driven into the basement parking lot, where he would be transferred to a wheelchair and taken upstairs to record, with Kiki lying quietly on the same table as the microphone, a bowl of fresh water nearby should he become thirsty.

Immediately on entering this facility, you are confronted by a huge blow-up of Welles in his signature black cape and matching wide-brimmed fedora, replete with a glowing endorsement of how much he has enjoyed working there. Judging solely by the appearance of the place, such high praise could be dismissed as standard Hollyweed bullshit. In the opening scene of *Who's Afraid of Virginia Woolf?*, Edward Albee references the famous Bette Davis quote, 'What a dump!' That, certainly, was my first impression. Then, I was passed along to the sound engineer who had recorded Welles before me. He, in turn, introduced me to the machines that made up his technical wizardry and explained how Welles had come to rely on them. First and foremost was an Aphex, or voice enhancer, which his apologists continue to insist that Welles had no need of, but which one has only to hear his hoarse and labored out-takes to know better. Another one of these machines was a time compressor, which made it possible to shave enough microseconds off a commercial so that his readings came in exactly on time – and without distorting them in the process.

The sad irony is that Orson Welles, who is characterized by his nearly preternatural mastery of the technology of the 1930s and '40s, in radio and the movies, would find himself, towards the end of his life, so hopelessly dependent on its latest incarnations.

As soon as my obligation to USC was over and done with, I loaded up my old Mazda wagon for the long drive back to Maine. I said my goodbyes to Mako and was sharing a few last moments with friends in the lobby of the Los Angeles Theatre Center when I was asked if I'd be interested in writing a one-man Orson Welles play. *Welles on Shakespeare* had just appeared and, frankly, I was 'Welles-ed out.'

'How about this?', someone volunteered. 'The actor's sitting in his dressing-room getting ready to play him.'

'That's it?'

'Well, he'll be talking, of course.'

'About what?'

'You're the writer; you tell me.'

The fellow proposing this was, of course, an actor – and a good one. His suggestion, on the other hand, was more in the order of a poetic notion rather than the basis of anything that could be developed into a plot.

Other than *Tru*, I couldn't think of a single one-character play that had held my attention from start to finish. Most often, their reliance on the notoriety of the character – be it Mark Twain or Paul Robeson or Gertrude Stein etc. – proved no substitute for that most basic of dramatic elements. Something to anticipate. An outcome worthy of the patience (and pocketbook) of its audience. (For me, the autobiographical collages by such performance artists as Anna Deavere Smith and the late Spalding Gray are grist for an altogether different set of conceits.)

Despite the attraction of finally writing something about Welles in his voice – *Welles on Shakespeare* and *The Theatre of Orson Welles* having been written in mine – without a viable plot, however truncated, this was not a project that I could see myself taking on.

My last stop before leaving LA was the recording studio where my engineer had prepared a going-away present for me: two audio cassettes made up of Welles' out-takes and open mike conversations (which, unbeknownst to Welles, he had also recorded). On the long drive back to Maine, I played and replayed these cassettes, literally dozens of times. Even the light-hearted moments, few and far between, were painful to listen to, as the voice coming over my speakers bore very little in common with the celebrated 'Voice of God' sound that we associate with him.

Yes, the work that went into my two books had left me with a wealth of material from which to flesh out the character of Orson Welles: his (and my) loathing of the academic mentality; how everyone in Hollyweed is constantly pimping for the people higher up the food chain; a passionate commitment to civil liberties that was second only to Eleanor Roosevelt (until the House Un-American Activities Committee chased him out of this country in 1947); and so forth.

When I drive long distance, especially after midnight when there is usually no traffic to speak of, I focus more on some problem that I'm trying to solve rather than the road ahead. (Think of it as a kind of mental cruise control; and, no, I've never had an accident – knock wood!) I knew that no matter how endlessly fascinating the character of Orson Welles could become, no matter that Welles himself was (arguably) the only humanist genius that America has ever produced, I was still confronted with the all-important question of what it was that set that particular day apart from the hundreds of other days that he spent in the shabby confines of that recording studio.

Until I could answer that question, I wouldn't have even the semblance of a plot.

Whatever else he may have been, Welles considered himself a director, first and foremost. And by May 7th, 1985, the day after his 70th and last birthday, the opportunity to direct another film had eluded him for over a dozen years. But thanks to the largesse of Steven Spielberg, who claimed to idolize Welles, this was to be the day when his long wait would finally be over.

The appalling mess that Tim Robbins made of Welles' 1937 stage triumph *The Cradle Will Rock*, and, most notably, the apparent glee he derived from portraying Welles himself as a drunken buffoon, took that project off the table. So, instead of films that Welles had hoped to make (such as his own version of *Cradle*, to star Spielberg's then-wife Amy Irving), I turned my attention to those films of his that he had yet to complete – above all, his cherished 'bambino,' *Don Quixote*.

The opposite of a 'Eureka!' moment has to be one that leaves you feeling like a damned fool for not having realised something before you finally did. In both practical and metaphorical terms *Don Quixote* was the ideal project to focus on and, despite their obvious differences in size, Welles enjoyed every bit the spiritual kinship with Cervantes' scrawny knight that he did with that other (and 'thrice wider') knight with whom he is so often identified – Falstaff.

Even Welles' boast 'How they'll miss me when I'm gone!', echoes Quixote's prophecy in Chapter II of the novel: 'O happy age, when my glorious deeds will be revealed to the world, deeds worthy of being engraved in bronze, sculpted in marble and painted in pictures for future generations.' Knowing this book as well as I do, I felt confident that I could identify enough significant passages to use throughout my play as asides (preferably recorded) by Welles to underscore the parallels between him and his fictional counterpart.

I spent the next several days after arriving back in Maine (safely, thank you) re-reading *Don Quixote* – and found more such passages than I could possibly have imagined.

Ten years and thirteen rewrites later, this is the Orson Welles play that is being published and/or performed from Argentina to France, from Mexico to Germany, from Spain to India (in Hindi), from Belgium to the Balkans, from Poland to Japan, and now the UK – almost everywhere, that is, but back here in the US.

From the well he is buried in, on the front lawn of the Ordóñez hacienda in Ronda, Spain, I can imagine Welles, ever the maverick, bellowing with laughter upon hearing this news – and giving the finger to this increasingly fucked-up country of ours.

Richard France

******

To my beloved wife, Elisabeth

This play received its world premiere as *Votre Serviteur, Orson Welles*, on 6th September 2006 at the Theatre Marigny in Paris with the following cast:

WELLES, Jean-Claude Drouot

MEL, Serge Le Lay

Translator, Jacques Collard

Director, Jean-Claude Drouot

Assistant Director, d'Alice Arpentinier

Sound, Michel Winogradoff

Set design, Sandrine Pelloquet

Costume design, Valerie Adda

Lighting, Emmanuel Drouot

The Spanish-language production opened at the 2008 Festival Grec in Barcelona, where it was selected as the Critics' Choice. After 18 months of touring, *Su Seguro Servidor, Orson Welles* reopened in October 2010 at the Teatro Bellas Artes in Madrid.

A second French-language production followed in November 2010 at the Theatre Jean Vilar in Belgium.

At the time of writing, the play has also been translated into another half-dozen languages, including Dutch, German, Portuguese and Romanian.

All is in darkness. Finally, we hear WELLES' voice. Gone is much of the flawless delivery and divine rumble we associate with his once incomparable voice. Instead, he sounds raspy and labored.

WELLES' VOICE: 'Build... repair... replenish. That's... what you'll be doing... when you feed your dog ... the complete nutrition... that's packed into a can... of Laddy Boy Premium Dog Food. This is Orson Welles... and I'm like... every other dog owner. Nothing... is too good... for my little Kiki. So... when my vet... assured me... that nothing went into... Laddy Boy... that we couldn't eat... ourselves... I decided to give it... a try. Laddy Boy... is specially formulated... for every stage in a dog's life. Like his master... Kiki... is getting along in years. So... I put him on Laddy Boy's... special... senior maintenance formula... for ageing dogs. How's this... for a mouth... watering... choice of selections? Apple meatloaf. Tamale pie. Salmon soufflé. And Kiki's... favourite... beef and bacon balls.'

OWNER'S VOICE: *(A Frank Perdue type.)* 'There's no difference between what's on my table and what goes into every can of my dog food.'

WELLES' VOICE: 'Laddy Boy... Premium... Dog Food. Your dog will love you... all the more... for it.'

A match is struck, revealing a fat bearded old man in a monk's habit lighting a huge cigar. He begins speaking to someone offstage.

WELLES: My name is George. Did you know that? True, it's only *one* of my names. But people become their names. George Welles?

He shudders at the thought. Lights up slowly as he blows out the match, revealing a recording studio: a chair and table, atop which is a phone, a reading stand and microphone. WELLES has a cane and a small cloth bag. He takes a puff or two on his cigar before continuing.

WELLES: Shaw's name was also George. Can you imagine *Saint Joan* or *Heartbreak House* or *Major Barbara* or any of those other marvelous plays being written by someone named George Shaw? *(Scoffs.)* Unthinkable! For that matter, can you imagine anyone named George being a producer and director on Broadway… an actor in motion pictures and on the legitimate stage… a writer and director of movies… a commentator on radio and television… a stage designer… a novelist… a cartoonist… a magician… a violinist… a pianist…

He turns to the audience, a mischievous smile on his face.

Isn't it remarkable: there are so many of me, and so few of you? *(Laughing along with them.)* That's how I introduced myself at a lecture I gave some years ago in Buffalo. They were having one of their hourly blizzards, and there were only a handful of people in the audience. You might say, I brought down the row with that line. *(More circumspect.)* I had no sooner come offstage than the house manager took me aside and said, 'There's a policeman waiting for you in your dressing room.' 'Don't go back to your hotel room', the officer warned me. 'Why not?' I asked. 'You're being set up. They've got an underage girl in your bed, and photographers waiting for you.' That's how determined our Mr. Hearst was to punish me for *Citizen Kane.*

WELLES' VOICE: I am he for whom are reserved all the most dangerous feats; but it causes my heart to burst with joy to tempt this peril, however great it may be.

WELLES: *(Upbeat again.)* They say you don't achieve true wisdom until the age of sixty. When I crossed that great divide, I emptied out my wardrobe and replaced most of it with six of these – the ultimate in comfort, especially for those of us who are… gastronomically challenged, I believe it's called today. Gastronomically challenged! Try saying that ten times in a row. I eat like Henry the Eighth… only I have better manners. My good friend, John Huston, had cast his father as Captain Ahab in *Moby Dick*. But Walter died before they could begin shooting. I'd enjoyed a great success as Ahab on the stage in London, so I called John to offer my services. *(Imitating John Huston.)* 'I'm afraid, Orson, I don't see you in Ahab's skin. There simply isn't room for *two* whales in *Moby Dick*.' I could always lose fifty pounds when I wanted to. I lost as much for *The Third Man*, and *twice* that for my AFI tribute a few years ago. Of course, I gained it all back… and then some. *(Puffs on his cigar.)* I love digressions, don't you? Read the first few pages of *Dead Souls* again, and you'll see how one mad little digression can enhance an ordinary narrative. So… here you have me – in the raw, as it were.

He lifts his habit to show his bare legs. MEL plays a few bars of 'The Stripper', which WELLES acknowledges. Music out. He covers up and surveys the audience, puffing contentedly on his cigar.

WELLES: *(Pointing.)* You, sir! You seem to be having trouble recognizing me. Could it have anything to do with my nose? Alas, this pudgy little thing is all the good lord, in his infinite wisdom, saw fit to endow me with. *(Sighs.)* Whatever was he thinking! Olivier's another one who hates his nose. One of the few beliefs we share in common is the importance of the nose in shaping an actor's approach to his role. *(Tweaking it.)* This tender button may do for comedy, but Larry and I are drawn to what is called in the classical French tradition, 'Kings' roles.' Lear.

Othello. Macbeth. *(Turning to demonstrate.)* Does this look to you like the profile to strike fear and pity in your hearts? *(Glowering at audience member.)* I was discussing my nose, sir. So, why are you staring at my... ampleur?

He scowls at this 'person' while taking a slow puff on his cigar. Finally, he relieves the tension with a laugh.

WELLES: Thought I meant it, didn't you? *(To the entire audience.)* My nose stopped growing before I entered my teens, by which time I was already over six feet tall. Rather than feel sorry for myself, I set about to improve on god's handiwork. How? Make-up. Movies, theater – I've always done my own. Over the years, I've accumulated several dozen false noses, each of which I fashioned myself – the height of the bridge, the flare of the nostrils, the length of the full organ – until I had the ideal proboscis in all its phallic splendor. I keep a number of them in a special box that I take with me when I'm called upon to go before the cameras. Whereupon, I clamp one on, cover it with greasepaint – *et voilà!* Falstaff... Harry Lime... Hank Quinlan.

He is jarred out of his reverie, first by a dog barking, then the screech of an audio tape being rewound.

WELLES: What in god's name is all that racket?

MEL'S VOICE: Be cool! I'm just applying some of my very own Mello Magic to that dog food spot you did earlier.

WELLES: *(Trying to remember.)* Dog food spot?

Sound out. MEL enters carrying a loose-leaf notebook and a separate sheet of paper.

WELLES: From the sound of it, you'd think you were engaging in some form of pagan ritual.

MEL hands the sheet of paper to him, then places the note-book on the reading stand, and exits. WELLES glances at the paper, then stands there, dejectedly, looking at his drab surroundings.

WELLES' VOICE: *(Breaking with sorrow.)* Here, my Sancho, shall I do my penance? Here shall the tears from my eyes swell in limpid streams, and here shall the sighs of my heart stir every mountain tree.

MEL'S VOICE: Give a listen to this.

We hear the completed Laddy Boy spot. MEL's machines have restored WELLES' voice and delivery to their legendary greatness.

So, how do ya like them apples?

WELLES: Too bad you didn't also think of me for the dog's part. That's how I started in this business, you know – as a D-Man.

MEL'S VOICE: A what?

WELLES: That was someone who could do dialects... accents... any kind of sound. Would you believe, I was the voice of the Dionne quintuplets when their births were announced on the radio?

MEL'S VOICE: You're puttin' me on!

WELLES: No, no; I was their coos and gurglings.

MEL'S VOICE: That's really far out! I mean, you doin' shit like that.

WELLES: *(Referring to the sheet of paper in his hand.)* Seems to me, I'm *still* doing shit, fifty years later. *(Crosses wearily to the chair.)* And still for the same reason: money, money, money!!!

He sits down and pauses to catch his breath before taking out a

77

thermos and appointment book from his cloth bag and placing them on the table. He puts on his glasses, locates a number in his book, and dials.

WELLES: *(Waits impatiently; brusquely.)* Alex! It's ten o'clock *(Listens.)* You're not still asleep, are you? *(Listens.)* Your appointment with Spielberg's at eleven. I want you in his office by a quarter to. I'll be at The Saloon for lunch. Meet me there. *(Listens.)* The Saloon, man! Of course Ma Maison. *(Listens.)* Where am I now? What kind of question is that? *(Listens.)* Yes, I had an early call this morning. A commercial for dog food. *(Listens.)* No, I didn't have to eat from the can, but I did have to celebrate its contents. Yes, I've fallen so low. *(Back to the matter at hand.)* Alex, the man is giving us a line of credit so we can finish *Don Quixote. (Heartfelt.) Mio bambino,* Alex – *mio bambino.* You of all people should know that. *(Listens.)* The negative is safe with Mauro in Rome. This time next week, we can be there too. *(Listens.)* How long have you worked for me? Thirty years? When have you ever known me to celebrate my birthday? *(Listens.)* And I wouldn't have last night either if it weren't for Steve and Amy. The party was their idea, not mine. *(Listens.)* I want you to know, I did my best dancing bear routine for that money. *(Listens; exasperated.)* You make it sound like I've pledged my soul to the devil. All he's asking… *(Listens; angrily.)* All he's asking is I have it ready to show at Cannes next year. *(Listens; puzzled.)* What do you mean, 'If I don't?' *(Amused.)* Then, I suppose the gates of hell will open thrice-wide for me. *(Listens.)* Alex, what am I? *(Listens.)* Yes, yes; but what am I above all else? *(Listens; as if to a child.)* And when was the last time anyone offered me a picture to direct? *(Listens; temper mounting.)* Anyone! Not just in this town! *(Listens.)* So, what would you have me do, twiddle my thumbs for *another* dozen years? Then, get your royal ass over to Spielberg's and bring that letter of credit to me at The Saloon… OR FIND YOURSELF ANOTHER MEAL TICKET!!!

He slams down the receiver. Pleased with himself, he unscrews the thermos and pours a cup of tea.

WELLES' VOICE: *(Expectantly.)* This, brother Panza, is the day when you shall see the boon that heaven has in store for me.

MEL enters, pushing a pole mike on wheels. WELLES is caught by surprise.

MEL: I just wanna change your mike.

WELLES: *(Warily.)* Will it make me sound any more like Orson Welles than the one I've been using?

MEL: That's what ya got the Mello Man for.

Carefully, he adjusts the mike so that it hangs over the reading stand and directly in front of WELLES' mouth.

MEL: *(Dismantling the table mike.)* Did I hear you say something about royalty?

WELLES: *(Coming around.)* Hmmm?

MEL: That guy… on the phone…

WELLES: *(Expansively.)* Prince Allesandro Tasca di Cuto.

MEL: A prince? You mean like Chuckie and Di?

WELLES: *(Warming to the subject.)* Better! He's a duke four times, a count three times, a marquis six times –

MEL: Cool!

WELLES: All it means is, he gets to keep his hat on when speaking with the King of Spain.

MEL: *(Hesitantly.)* Right... *(A pause.)* So you're finally gonna finish it.

WELLES: Ummm...

MEL: Do you know, you've been workin' on that film longer than I've been alive?

WELLES: *(Sarcastically.)* All the more reason to get it right this time.

MEL: An' The Man himself's puttin' up the do-re-me.

WELLES: *(As before.)* Yes, I'm one lucky hombre.

WELLES' VOICE: Leave everything to god, friend Sancho, and he will give us what is most fitting.

MEL: They showed that at school.

WELLES: They showed *what* at school?

MEL: *Don Quixote.* My professor has a print.

WELLES: Your professor goes around stealing other people's property, does he? Some role model you have there!

MEL: A guy in the Valley was sellin' them. Quality sucks. Gotta be tenth generation.

WELLES: Well... that's some consolation.

MEL: Didn't I read about you usin' that kid, what the hell's her name?

WELLES: Patty McCormack.

MEL: Yeah! I saw you, but I didn't see her. She get left on the cuttin' room floor?

WELLES: *(Flaring up.)* You're only talking about the most gifted child star since Liz Taylor.

MEL: Whoa! No offense! So what happened to her?

WELLES: *(Sadly.)* I ran out of money before I could finish her scenes. It was two years before I could resume production.

MEL: *(Sympathetic.)* And by that time…

WELLES: By that time she's grown up.

MEL: Bummer! *(Pause.)* I know what I'd do.

WELLES: *(Amused.)* What you'd do! And what, may I ask, is that?

MEL: *(Warily.)* Shoot around her.

WELLES: Now, why didn't *I* think of that? *(Meaning the note-book.)* Soon as we're through here, I'll take myself down to *The Hollywood Reporter* and run an ad. *(As if reading a headline.)* 'Wanted: Twelve Year Old Actress with the talent of a Patty McCormack.'

MEL: That isn't what I meant.

WELLES: No? Then, what *did* you mean?

MEL: Shoot everything but her face. Like Ed Wood did in *Plan 9 from Outer Space* when Béla Lugosi died on him.

WELLES: I'm afraid I don't know that one.

MEL: Worst piece of shit ever made.

WELLES: I'd like to think I've set my sights a little higher than that. *(Long pause; confidingly.)* Actually, I was planning to reshoot those scenes with my daughter, Beatrice.

MEL: Can she act?

WELLES: *(Laughing.)* I'm sure I could have coaxed a performance out of her. But there, too, 'the noiseless foot of time crept swiftly by.' *(Pause.)* I hate admitting this, but I've forgotten your name.

MEL: *(With a flourish.)* The Mello Man, at your service! Mel for short.

WELLES: I turned seventy yesterday, Mel.

MEL: No shit! *(Catching himself.)* Hey, I didn't mean any disrespect.

WELLES: No shit is right! Seventy years old. *(Sips his tea; thoughtfully.)* No longer the Boy Wonder, that's for sure.

MEL attaches a filter to the mike, makes sure of the alignment with WELLES' mouth, then steps back to admire his handiwork.

MEL: *(Starting off; then.)* Do you mind my askin'… *(Thinks better of it.)* No, better not.

WELLES: Asking what?

MEL: Well… my professor said –

WELLES: Would that be the same thief you mentioned before?

MEL: He said you made that *Quixote* flick with your own money.

WELLES: *Quixote. Othello. F for Fake.* Who can remember them all?

The change of lighting that accompanies WELLES' reverie also allows MEL to fade away. WELLES comes downstage to the audience.

No studio would back me. I couldn't even get a loan from the bank. Unless you're a Spielberg or a Lucas, you can expect to spend more time putting the deal together than you will making the movie. College boys from NYU or USC or AFI! They sit around their boardrooms and speak in code. Points. Market share. Feasibility analysis. Snot-nosed little shits! It used to be... *(As if speaking on the phone.)* Orson Welles for Darryl Zanuck, please. *(To audience.)* He used to put me through my dancing bear routine, but in the end... *(On the phone; very effusive.)* Darryl! What a joy it is to hear a friendly voice for a change! *(Listens.)* I have all these people over here yelling at me – in Italian, no less. There's this little matter of a hotel bill I've run up. *(Listens.)* Yes, they're still with me, the whole company on full pension. *(Listens.)* If I do that, I can't be sure of getting them back when I need them. And if I'm ever going to finish this picture, I'd damned well... *(Listens.)* Don't you think I haven't already thought of that? *(Pouring it on.)* The *Carabinieri* are getting ready to storm the hotel. And the only other way out of here is to jump in the canal. *(Falls to his knees; playfully.)* Darryl, please! I'm on my knees to you. Save us! No-one else can. It's you or... *(His voice cracking.)* a watery grave. *(Thoroughly enjoying this shared pretence.)* You wouldn't want that on your conscience, would you?

He nods confidently to the audience, gets to his feet, and takes a puff or two on his cigar.

WELLES: A hundred thousand should save the day. *(Listens.)* You still want me for *The Black Rose*, don't you? What do you think that's going to cost you? *(Listens.)* Good! Have your man wire the money to me here at the Colombe d'Or. Bye, Darryl! Bye, now!

The lights change back, as he returns to the studio and sits down.

Don't get the wrong idea: they were all monsters...

the Zanucks... the Warners... the Harry Cohns. But they were also devoted to this business. Sam Goldwyn invited me onto the set of *Wuthering Heights,* and I said something like, 'What a good film Willie Wyler's making.' Goldwyn turned on me: '*I'm* making *Wuthering Heights.* Wyler's only directing it.' *(A more somber reflection.)* There's none of that spirit anymore. I'm not even sure Hollywood deserves to be called a movie town anymore. Maybe the industry's exhausted itself. When I was starting out, colour was all the rage. *(Mischievously.)* Of course, I ignored it. *(To his target in the audience.)* That surprises you? *(To everyone else.)* Are there any mavericks in the audience? *(Finds one.)* Acquaint him with our breed, would you please? *(Back to his story.)* Then they came up with Cinerama... or CinemaScope. Now, everyone is worshipping at the altar of computer graphics. But through it all, what has mattered most to the audience? In my day all they cared about was whether Veronica Lake's hair was all her own – the same question that's asked today of Burt Reynolds. *(His devilish smile.)* The answer is yes... and no. Which is which? My lips are sealed. *(Again serious.)* I hope this doesn't sound like sour grapes. Hollywood is Hollywood. Whatever your luck – and I've had the very best luck, and the very worst luck – no-one forces you to sit down and join the game, so none of us has the right to be bitter. *(Puffs thoughtfully.)* I was merely... questioning the wisdom of my decision. People have the wrong idea about Hollywood. Behind all its phony tinsel lies... the *real* tinsel. *(Another puff.)* If I'd had any sense, I would have left this business years ago –

MEL'S VOICE: How 'bout we get started on –

WELLES: Right after *Kane*. Returned to the theatre. Become a writer. Gone into politics, as the president, Mr. Roosevelt, wanted me to. No, not a writer. I couldn't stand that awful silence when you wind up a chapter – and the typewriter doesn't burst into applause. *(To MEL.)* Do you know what I dreamed of becoming as a child?

MEL'S VOICE: What's that?

WELLES: A painter.

MEL'S VOICE: Okay…

WELLES: I wonder if I shouldn't have kept at it? As a painter, you get up in the morning, clean your brushes, and go to work. How expensive can a box of paints be? Nothing compared to my box of paints as a filmmaker. And I have to go begging for every last cent of it. *(A fond remembrance.)* You never know where that can lead you. I was back in Venice, raising money for some project or other. My pigeon was a sinister-looking Russian who was said to be worth a billion dollars. As luck would have it, Winston Churchill was staying at the same hotel. You *do* know who I'm talking about.

MEL'S VOICE: *(Playing along.)* Churchill! Churchill! Where do I know that name? Right! It's on those cigars of yours.

WELLES: *(Taken in; shocked.)* Dear god!!!

MEL'S VOICE: I was just pullin' your chain. Of course I know who Churchill was.

WELLES: I would hope so. If he and FDR hadn't been there to guide us through the war, our world would be a very different place today.

MEL'S VOICE: Better or worse? *(Before WELLES can explode.)* Okay, okay! *(Imitating Churchill.)* 'We shall fight them on the beaches, an' in the air, an'…' whatever. Do I know my history, or what?

WELLES: *(Mollified.)* Close enough. Anyway, we came down to lunch one afternoon, my pigeon and I, and there he was. As we passed his table, Churchill nodded to me. Mr. Roosevelt had introduced us during the war, and Churchill had come to see my *Othello* some years after. 'Citizen Coon', as the critics called it. *(Chuckling.)* Seems I'd made myself up too black for their taste. This made a big impression on my Russian. 'Good heavens,' he said, 'Sir Winston knows you.' 'Of course,' I answered nonchalantly. The next morning, I went for a swim and found myself on the beach next to Churchill. 'You don't know the good you did me when I came into the dining-room with that fellow yesterday,' I said. 'I'm in Venice to raise money for my new film, and your nodding to me at lunch… well, sir, you have no idea how helpful that was.' Churchill didn't say anything. He was practically deaf, so you never knew if he'd heard you or not. I thanked him and excused myself to dress for dinner. At the appointed hour, I met my pigeon, with whom I was still negotiating, and we went into the dining room. And, once again, there was Churchill. As we passed his table, he took hold of my arm and called out, 'Most potent and reverent signiors, my very noble and approv'd good masters…'

Othello's lines! The old fox *had* heard me. Before the day was over, I was on a plane back to Rome, with a certified check in my pocket. That was a happy exception. More often, I do my dancing bear over lunch at The Saloon. My pigeon is from the world of business with dreams of striking it rich here in

Hollywood. So, I'll fill his head full of stories about *Kane*... or the Martian broadcast... or what it was like to be married to Rita Hayworth... things my 'learned *(With absolute contempt.)* bee-ographers' have somehow managed to overlook. My starry-eyed pigeon will say something like 'I'll have my lawyers draw up the agreement, and get back to you next week.'

MEL'S VOICE: I think we oughta do that All American spot first, then the EDS promo for that rich dude in Dallas.

WELLES: If only you knew how many 'next weeks' there've been these past dozen years.

He puts down his cigar, opens the note-book and turns to the right page.

How many of these All American spots did you say we were doing?

MEL'S VOICE: Just the one.

WELLES: Then, why do I have two pieces of copy, two very *different* pieces of copy?

MEL'S VOICE: *(Nervously.)* They're not sure which one they wanna to go with... an'... well, they'd like to hear both.

WELLES: Let me see if I understand you. I'm being asked to read *both* pieces of copy, but our sponsor is only willing to pay me for one of them?

MEL'S VOICE: *(As before.)* Somethin' like that...

WELLES: I don't do free-bees – unless, of course, they're a charitable organization... in which case I'll want to see proof of their non-profit status.

No response from MEL.

(Finally.) So... we'll just have to make up their minds for them...

No response.

Won't we?

MEL'S VOICE: *(Resigned.)* Guess so...

WELLES puts on his glasses and examines both pieces of copy, clearing his throat as he makes his choice.

WELLES: Any time...

MEL'S VOICE: I need a level first.

WELLES: *(Again sounding labored as he reads.)* 'There's a change... on the horizon. Is your... business... prepared?'

MEL'S VOICE: Can you... pick it up any? *(WELLES nods as he takes a sip of tea.)* All American Financial. Take one.

WELLES: *(As before.)* 'There's a change... on the horizon. Is your... business... prepared? At... All American Financial... we provide... the types of programs... that keep people... and organizations... moving... towards long-term financial success... come what may. All American Financial... supporting... the whole idea... of financial... independence... for over one hundred years.' *(Thumbing through the copy in his note-book.)* What time are my Japanese expected?

MEL'S VOICE: They're down for three o'clock.

WELLES: And you expect me to read all this beforehand? I won't have any voice left by then.

MEL'S VOICE: No problemo! Remember that newspaper spot we did the other day?

WELLES: *(Drawing a blank.)* Newspaper spot?

MEL plays the unenhanced version so WELLES can hear for himself how badly his once incomparable voice has deteriorated. WELLES is horrified.

WELLES ON TAPE: 'In the forest… of Mexico… Mayan farmers… use axes and machetes… to clear… and scorch… the land.'

WELLES' VOICE: *(Utterly mournful.)* O star of my fortune, witness the pass to which I have come.

MEL: *(Pretending to be surprised.)* How the hell…..? Hey, man, I'm sorry. This is what I wanted you to hear.

He now plays the finished version, replete with birds chirping and the wind blowing. We hear the WELLES voice and delivery of legend.

WELLES ON TAPE: 'In the forests of Mexico, Mayan farmers use axes and machetes to clear and scorch the land. They do not replant what they have destroyed. Fifteen hundred miles away, in Michigan, shopping malls and industrial parks have begun fragmenting the woodlands. Our forests are turning into concrete jungles right before our eyes. What these two events have in common may be surprising – especially if you're a songbird. Look for this series in the *Detroit Free Press*.'

MEL'S VOICE: *(Smugly understated.)* The Mello Man, at your service! *(Anticipating the question.)* I just ran you through my Aphex.

WELLES: *(Scrambling for pen and paper.)* Your what?

MEL'S VOICE: A machine that enhances the voice.

WELLES: *(Truly impressed.)* I'll say it does! What's the name again?

MEL'S VOICE: *(As WELLES writes it down.)* A-P-H-E-X. Say you're doin' a sixty, an' you come in four, five seconds long. I got me another machine in here that can shave enough microseconds off each syllable so it sounds like you nailed that sucker flat.

WELLES: And what is that called?

MEL'S VOICE: A time compressor.

WELLES: *(Writing it down.)* Let me see if I understand you. No matter how I may actually sound, or how slowly I read this stuff, those gadgets of yours –

MEL'S VOICE: Can give you back that famous Voice of God sound of yours.

WELLES: Every time?

MEL'S VOICE: Every time.

WELLES: *(Awestruck.)* Did I not tell thee, Sancho, how everything that happens in this place is done by enchantment?

MEL'S VOICE: *(Openly smug.)* With what I got in here, I can make a mouse fart sound like the Mormon Tabernacle Choir.

WELLES leans back in his chair and lets out a great sigh of relief.

WELLES: No more take after take! *(Holds up a piece of paper.)* All I have to do is read this once… *(Lets it float to the floor.)* and abracadabra!!!

MEL'S VOICE: *(Hedging his bet.)* Ummm… pretty much.

WELLES: *(Almost giddy.)* I can almost feel the years falling off me. Do you know how I came to be known as the Boy Wonder?

MEL'S VOICE: They got tired of callin' you a genius all the time?

WELLES: A genius in Hollywood parlance is someone who is either dead or otherwise unavailable. I am neither. No… there've only been two people in this business worthy of that distinction, Chaplin and D.W. Griffith. With me, it was more a matter of being in the right place at the right time when the right technology became available. *(Confiding in him.)* Would you like to know why Gregg Toland offered to shoot *Kane* for me?

MEL'S VOICE: *(Eagerly.)* And how!

WELLES: I'd never made a film before, so I didn't know what was impossible. I thought the camera could capture anything the eye could see. *(Laughing.)* Ignorance! Sheer ignorance! That's what excited him. *(Imitating Toland.)* 'There isn't anything about the camera that I can't teach you in an afternoon.' And he did. 'Now tell me how you want this picture to look,' he said. Watching him on the set – the way he positioned the camera, chose his lenses, framed each shot – I apprenticed with Rembrandt. *(Back to the matter at hand.)* So, my young Houdini, what would you have me do?

MEL'S VOICE: Just start readin'.

WELLES takes another sip of tea and clears his voice as he locates the right page in the notebook.

WELLES: *(Again labored.)* The world… a rather… awesome space. Fifty-seven million… square miles of land. Somewhere down there… sits a business. Maybe… it's a bank. A convenience store. No matter… what it may be… there's… another company… that knows more about it… than you could possibly… imagine. More… about its location.

More about its... customer preferences... than even its managers do. That company... is EDS Electronic... Data Systems.'

Sound of the tape rewinding. He thinks of something that causes him to chuckle.

I was all of eighteen when I began in this business. Radio was to actors of the thirties what soaps are today – grocery money. We held our noses all the way to the bank. I was also directing *The Voodoo Macbeth* in Harlem. We'd rehearse from midnight till six in the morning. Then, I'd shower and rush downtown to do *The March of Time... Peter Absolute... The Wonder Show. (Shaking his head.)* God only knows what else! I'd dash from one station to the other. They'd hand me a script, and I'd ask, 'What's the character?' 'An eighty-year-old Chinaman,' they'd say. I'd do the eighty-year-old Chinaman, then hurry to my next assignment. Have you ever tried getting around Manhattan by cab? And I never had a moment to spare. So I hit upon the idea of using an ambulance. I could do that because there was no law in New York that said you had to be sick to ride in an ambulance. I was making something like two thousand a week as an anonymous radio actor when CBS offered me the lead in a new mystery series.

We hear the signature tag line, replete with laughter, for The Shadow. *'The weed of crime bears bitter fruit. The Shadow knows.'*

So... I became The Shadow on radio... and directed *Doctor Faustus* for the WPA – *and* played the lead. *The Shadow* ended at eight-thirty, just as the curtain was going up on *Faustus*. I'd deliver my last line, then run out the door and into my ambulance. He'd race across town, his klaxon clearing the way, while I changed into my costume. And do you know, I never once missed my cue. Not one time!

He pauses to remember this great triumph of his youth.

WELLES' VOICE: Is this the face that launched a thousand ships

And burnt the topless towers of Ilium?

Sweet Helen, make me immortal with a kiss.

WELLES: I've done so many commercial endorsements over the years that I couldn't begin to remember them all. *(As if holding up a glass.)* 'We will sell no wine before its time.' The Paul Masson people must have thought I was still downing the stuff when they hired me. *(Pleased with himself.)* Took them three years to learn otherwise. I was getting ready for my AFI tribute when Merv Griffin happened to mention how svelte I looked. *(Imitating Griffin.)* 'To what do you attribute your recent loss of weight, Orson?' I answered, simply, that I'd stopped snacking, and no longer drank alcohol. You can imagine how that went over with Paul Masson. They used their new line of light wines to replace me with Johnny Gielgud. I believe this was his first commercial endorsement, and he was none too pleased with it. With the money, yes; but not the product. *(An overly fey imitation of Gielgud.)* 'I assure you, Orson…' The trouble with affecting an English accent is that, to our ears, they all sound like fairies. 'I assure you, Orson, they came to me, *not* the other way around.' 'No need to explain, John.' 'I still consider *Chimes* the finest Shakespeare ever filmed. But you musn't tell Larry. You know how easily threatened he gets.' 'Oh yes, John, I know all too well.'

WELLES' VOICE: Villain! You have bloodied me to a pulp – and all out of envy because I am your only rival in feats of valor.

WELLES: 'Ralph wouldn't like my saying this, but I can't imagine a better Falstaff than yours, Orson. And that you should think of me for King Henry... well, I shall always be grateful.' 'No-one, John – not Ralph, and certainly not Larry – could have played it half as well.' 'I have a confession to make, Orson.' 'Oh! And what is that, John?' 'I don't drink their wine, either. They poured me a glass of the Colombard – which I pretended to like. But between you and me, Orson... this *will* stay between you and me, I hope.' 'My lips are sealed, John.' 'I thought it very... nondescript. No, that's not the word for it.' 'Try innocuous, John.' 'Exactly! I can't imagine anyone ordering Paul Masson off a wine list, certainly not at any restaurant that you and I might frequent.' Clearly, Johnny G. was missing the point. 'Think of commercial work as grocery money', I told him, 'not the damnation of Faust.' 'You do a lot of it then?' he asked. *(The phone rings.)* I allowed as how I did. 'Where do you draw the line, Orson?' *(Another ring.)* 'I'm not sure I follow you, John.' 'I mean, is there any product you *wouldn't* speak for?

The phone is picked up mid-ring offstage by MEL. WELLES looks at the copy in his hand, then crumples it in disgust. MEL enters.

MEL: You doin' your magic act on the Carson show later this week?

WELLES: And what if I am?

MEL: He says ta tell you he's the guy that sent you the watch –

WELLES: *(Eagerly.)* That keeps perfect time! Yes, I need to speak with him! *(On the phone; gushing charm.)* Richard! How good of you to call. *(Listens.)* Alas, I left the watch at home. Any chance of your calling

me there tonight? I made a mess of your thirty-seven
gag the last time I did his show, and our Johnny can
be very unforgiving when things go wrong. So, if
you could just talk me through it tonight... *(Listens.)*
That's it? And you wonder why I call you the Edison
of magic! I see what's-his-name is giving me the high
sign from the booth.

MEL: I'm doin' what?

*WELLES is surprised to see that MEL is still in the studio and
gestures for him to leave. MEL exits.*

WELLES: I have a client coming in from Japan this
afternoon, and I have to wade through endless
dribble before they arrive. *(Thumbing through the copy
as he listens.)* Yes, they do love to visit Hollywood.
(Listens.) I'm reading a dozen of my favourite short
stories. *(Listens.)* In English, yes. Guess what? I've
finally managed to raise the last few dollars I need
to finish *Don Quixote. (Listens.)* I know, I know. But
we're not talking just any old pigeon this time. It's
Mr. Hollywood himself! *(Listens.)* Spielberg, dear
boy – Spielberg!!! *(Listens; defensively.)* What do you
mean, 'given up'? *(Listens.)* You sound just like Alex.
Richard, the man idolizes me! *(Listens.)* No, *Quixote*
is not his kind of movie. *(Listens.)* I don't disagree.
But you've got to admit, nobody's ever milked
that purity-in-peril formula better than our Steven.
(Listens.) Of course it's schlock, the gold standard of
schlock that everyone in this town would kill their
firstborn to duplicate. Well... *almost* everyone. There
are still a few of us who've managed to avoid the
cookie cutter. Now, I really must be getting back
to work. But you will be sure to call me tonight?
(Listens.) Good. *(Listens.)* Good. Talk to you then.

*He hangs up, comes downstage to a magician's table, and
locates a cigar. With that devilish smile of his, he gets out a*

blowtorch and lights up with a flourish.

WELLES: I was six when I saw my first magic show.
Any time a Thurston… Blackstone… Long Tack Sam
would come to Chicago, my father would gather up
my brother, Dickie, and me, and off we'd go to see
them. Houdini was my first teacher. He was a friend
of my father's; so, I was taken around to his dressing-
room. And my father said, 'The boy wants to be a
magician.' 'Fine! I'll teach him,' Harry said.

He finds a large ball and levitates it.

In vaudeville, there were long waits between shows.
If Harry didn't have company, he would demonstrate
various effects.

He takes a hoop and passes it around the floating ball.

And he gave me a piece of advice that's still reflected
in everything I do. A performance, he told me, is
made up of two things: out front, where the audience
gets to see the intended effect; and backstage, where
the wires are.

CIRCUS BARKER: *(Loud and expansive.)* Ladies and
gentlemen! Welcome… to the Mercury Wonder
Show!

*WELLES stands there, lost in his reverie. But for his follow-
spot, the stage goes dark.*

Starring… Princess Rita… Jo-Jo the Clown…
Calliope Aggie… and the one, the only, Orson the
Magnificent!!!

WELLES: *(Bowing to the audience.)* I am *Doctor* Welles, if
you please: DDT, LSD, STP.

CIRCUS BARKER: See Jo-Jo, the human sewing machine! Calliope Aggie, the girl with the x-ray vision! See Princess Rita sawed in half – and live to tell about it!

WELLES: Alas, not Princess Rita, I'm afraid.

CIRCUS BARKER: But due to the terrible strain on the practitioners of these miraculous effects –

WELLES: To say nothing of studio interference –

CIRCUS BARKER: The management reserves the right to alter the program without prior notice.

WELLES: In those days, actors were owned by their studios. *(Laughing.)* They called it 'being under contract.' That could mean anything. Fox had poor Marilyn Monroe spending more time on her back than before the camera. Rita was the property of Mr. Harry Cohn at Columbia. And Harry was adamant – a chronic condition with him – that Rita quit our nightly entertainments. *(Imitating Cohn.)* 'I'm payin' you all that money to be a star, an' you're performin' for nothin' in a tent with that nutcase? *(Indicating that he is the nutcase in question.)* Over my dead body!' So, I never did get to saw Rita in half. Marlene Dietrich heard what happened and offered to fill in. *(Imitating Dietrich.)* 'Orson', she asked… for the benefit of the audience, of course… 'how does zis treek work?' *(A drum roll begins offstage, getting louder and louder.)* To which I answered, saw in hand, 'Just you wait, Marlene. This will kill you.'

CIRCUS BARKER: *(Booming and ominous.)* Twelve… Have Died!

WELLES: The bullet catch! In full view of the audience, too. And at least that many more have been wounded. The bullet catch is the most dangerous effect in all of magic. Even Houdini, as fearless as he was, wouldn't risk it.

CIRCUS BARKER: *(Bigger than before.)* TWELVE... HAVE DIED!!!

WELLES: Long Beach was the port of embarkation for our boys going off to fight the Pacific War. Before they shipped out, they usually managed a visit to Hollywood. I thought the least I could do was gather up my friends and entertain them. If they were shy about asking Rita to have their picture taken with them, you should have seen them with Marlene. She was old enough to be their mother, but you'd never know it to see her in those skin-tight gowns of hers. And when she kissed them, they all but peed their pants. When I announced the bullet catch, the tent was packed – and not just with our boys in uniform. Our Mr. Hearst was still after my scalp. So, his minions – Harry Cohn, Louella Parsons, Louis B. Mayer – they turned out in droves... no doubt, hoping to witness number thirteen.

He puts down his cigar and, in the most exaggerated manner, begins to exercise his mouth: first, by opening and closing it as widely as possible; then, clamping his teeth together. Finally, he spits in his hands, rubs them together, and takes a position to catch the bullet.

Ladies and gentlemen, for this illusion I require the assistance of a marksman at the back of the theater.

The drum roll reaches a crescendo. Then... silence. We hear a bullet being slammed into the breach of a rifle. This is followed by an even longer and more agonizing silence. Finally, a shot is fired. WELLES' head snaps back, as if wounded. A rivulet of blood trickles down his chin. Slowly, he recovers, wiping away the blood, showing the bullet between his teeth. He holds it up for all to see.

WELLES: Can you imagine Clark Gable doing this, with his dentures?

He retrieves his cigar and, smiling, drops the bullet into the ashtray. It lands with a clank.

MEL'S VOICE: Are we here ta work or what?

WELLES: Coming! I'm coming, dammit! I arrived out here at a time that has become legendary. I was all of twenty-four at the time. The war hadn't started and everyone was still here, all those famous names, still giving their marvelous parties! It was a sort of *Götterdämmerung* moment. Garbo was my next door neighbor. She didn't have a pool. So, every Sunday morning, from ten to eleven, I let her use mine. I was expected to wait inside, with the curtains closed, till the last splash was heard. It wasn't that she was naked or anything; she simply didn't want anyone looking at her. Well, I soon tired of that, and went in swimming with her. There we were, Garbo and I, passing the rubber ring back and forth, when the news about Pearl Harbor came over the radio. I love my country, god knows; but I didn't want to be drafted into the Army. With my lack of formal education, I would have served my time as a mere footsoldier. So, my childhood guardian, Dr. Bernstein, in his capacity as a specialist in such things, petitioned the draft board to have me classified 4-F. *(Amused.)* To hear him tell it, I was suffering from chronic myelitis, original syndrome arthritis, bronchial asthma – and, best of all, inverted flat feet. That was all the excuse our Mr. Hearst needed to label me a Soviet agent, as well as a draft dodger, in all his subject newspapers. He based that

charge on the fact that Dr. Bernstein had been born
in Russia. My legal guardian, mind you; *not* my
biological father! *(Mischievously.)* Do you know what
really infuriated him about *Citizen Kane*? The word
'Rosebud'. It was his pet name for Marion Davies'
… *(Relishing each syllable.)* pu-den-da! I was visited
by a member of the House Un-American Activities
Committee. He wanted to know if, in fact, I *was*
a communist. In those days, accusing someone of
being a communist was like playing the race card
today. Sheer demagoguery! You were immediately
put on the defensive. Except Bogart, god bless him!
(Imitating an angry Bogart.) 'C'mon, admit it! You
bastards are out to nail anyone who's ever scratched
his ass during the National Anthem.' I asked my
inquisitor what he meant by a communist. 'Someone
who gives his money to the government,' he said.
Well, by that definition, I was eighty-five percent
communist; that's how much I was paying in taxes.
But the other fifteen percent, I assured him, was
thoroughly capitalistic. I can make light of it now,
but the blacklist was just around the corner. We like
to think the one-two punch of HUAC and McCarthy
did us in. But that wasn't until after the war, when
the right wing came out of their wormholes with a
vengence. That horse's ass with the sunny disposition
we now have in the White House, and his doe-eyed
cadaver of a wife, are the latest examples – with
the worst of their kind yet to come. *(Still feeling the
betrayal.)* No… as those shameful hearings made so
painfully clear, the rot was within. *(With loathing.)*
Adolphe Menjou and Robert Taylor wrapping
themselves in the flag before the Committee – it was
all I could do to keep from vomiting. *(Sadly.)* There
were very few of us who didn't betray our position…
who didn't name names. I'd like to think that,
had I stayed on here in Hollywood, I would have

behaved better than so many of my 'liberal' friends, who turned on each other to keep themselves in swimming pools. *(To MEL.)* Where are we?

MEL'S VOICE: Let's knock off that beer spot first, then –

WELLES: *(Having located it.)* Ready?

MEL'S VOICE: When have I *not* been?

WELLES: *(Clears his throat.)* This imported beer... is everything... you'd expect. It has a rich... full-bodied... imported taste... as you'd expect. But here's one thing... you wouldn't... expect. It's light. Amstel Light Bier. Imported by... Van Munching... and Company... New York.' *(Waits for a response from MEL; finally.)* Well?

MEL'S VOICE: Gimme a minute to play with it.

WELLES: Play with what? Oh, you mean those machines of yours.

MEL'S VOICE: *(Over the sound of rewinding.)* Exactamondo!!!

WELLES: Go for it! *(He takes a puff on his cigar.)* Like my father, I spent my twenties in tireless pursuit of dancers. In his case, it was showgirls. My own tastes ran more towards ballerinas. Mind you: I was never the sexual acrobat Chaplin was – or Warren Beatty still is. I lived by the motto, 'Once a king, always a king. But once a night... is quite enough, thank you.' Normally, when I meet someone for the first time, all they want to talk about is my movies – how I got this shot in *Kane*, or that shot in *Touch of Evil*. Not Warren. Almost the first question he asked me was, 'How can you tell if a girl spits or swallows?' I'd been cautioned beforehand that he thinks of nothing else, day or night, so the question didn't catch me unawares. 'Look at her fingernails,' I told

him. 'If they're healthy, it's a good bet she swallows.'
He still enjoys reminding me how well that advice
has served him over the years. People forget I was
once leading man material myself. Kane. Rochester.
Harry Lime. My high skinny years, I call them.
(Raising himself out of the chair.) From that... to this!
I believe it was Aristotle who said, 'Gluttony is a
positive virtue; it celebrates the best things in life.'
Or words to that effect. A positive virtue? *(Disgusted
with himself.)* I need the driver to help me into his
cab – and *two* people to help me get out. I can't
tie my own shoelaces; my man, Freddy, has to do
it for me. I live with the most desirable woman in
town, but I can't even remember the last time I was
able to make love to her. In *A Man for All Seasons,* to
squeeze me behind that desk, I had to be lowered
by crane. And when we were finished shooting, the
same crane raised me out of there. *(Laughs suddenly.)*
They also saw fit to provide me with a bedpan to
pee into between takes. *(Puffing on his cigar.)* Better
to empty something like that than hoist me up and
down every time Mother Nature called. *(In a better
mood.)* I was equally popular with my own sex. I had
what the Irish actor, Mícheál MacLiammóir, referred
to as 'disconcerting Chinese eyes.' They were to
him, anyway. I had that chorus boy look about me.
Older gentlemen wanting to further my career, or
talk to me about poetry – I got on to that early in
life. I became a sort of Lillie Langtry with the older
homosexual set. I never insulted anyone. Instead, I'd
put them off the way girls do when you take them
home with certain expectations after a night on the
town. I'd say, 'I've developed this terrible headache
and need to lie down... alone.' They pretty much
left me alone once they realised I wasn't inclined
in their direction. *(Grunts.)* Except Houseman! Old
Jocko! There was never any let-up with him – from

the day he 'discovered' me, quote-unquote, until we opened *The Voodoo Macbeth*. I was playing Tybalt to Katherine Cornell's geriatric Juliet, and was sitting in my dressing room waiting for the play to end so I could take my curtain call. It was broiling hot backstage, and I was stripped to the waist. You know how you can sense when someone's watching you? I looked up… and there he was. *(Imitating Houseman.)* 'Mr. Welles? I am John Houseman.' The purpose of his visit, or so he said, was to offer me the lead in a new play. Of course he'd already been turned down by the likes of Paul Muni… Alfred Lunt… John Barrymore… all the great stars of the day, and the right *age* for the role. I suppose, at the ripe old age of nineteen, I was the logical alternative.

WELLES' VOICE: *(Warily.)* No soft words for me; I know thee well.

WELLES: Houseman kept running his eyes over my body as we talked. It was like being backstage again with Micheál at the Gate. I made a mistake in Dublin, and it cost me dearly. After my initial success, he rewarded me – if that's the right word for it – with smaller and smaller roles. I was still the eager school-boy, after all, and not the least bit stand-offish. No wonder Micheál soon lost interest in me. *(With impish wickedness.)* So, I made up my mind with Houseman – to torture him. I was living in a one-room tenement on Riverside Drive. The bathtub was in the middle of the room. At night, I put a board over it, and it became my bed. Houseman had just been appointed head of the Negro Theater Project and was looking for a director to take up to Harlem with him. Mind you, he'd never seen anything I'd directed. On what, then, could he base his unquestioning faith in my talent? *(Relishing the memory.)* The time had come to give him a glimpse. So, I filled the tub with water and climbed in. I was still lying there when he arrived, my gigantic proportions – his choice of words, not mine – my gigantic proportions on full display. I stood up to show him that my... bulk... owed nothing to refraction, that I was just as – how did he put it – Enormous! I was just as enormous outside the tub as in. He gulped and asked what play I'd like to direct. I said *Macbeth*. He said, 'Fine.' And I was on the payroll. Our time together in Harlem was not without incident. I had to put up with being called his boyfriend, an impression he did nothing to correct. He'd come up to me and say... *(Imitating Houseman.)* 'You know, Orson, I had the most delicious dream about you last night.' I was sitting in my office at the theater, just reading a book. Houseman came in and asked who it was written by. I told him, Gertrude Stein. 'You realise, of course,' he said, 'that she was the beneficiary of the lesbian network in Paris, just as your career is benefiting greatly from your association with my friends and me here in New York.' Before I could say anything, he'd turned on his heel and stormed out the door. People think racial tensions are only something that's come about in the past few years. We faced it every day we were in Harlem. The atmosphere during rehearsals was one of wild hatred. The Communist Party in Harlem was telling people that Houseman was letting his 'boyfriend' prepare a burlesque of *Macbeth*. Why else were we using witch doctors and voodoo drummers? There's none of that in Shakespeare. No amount of assurance on our part could get them to believe that we were in Harlem for any other purpose than to ridicule the Negro. Then, on opening night, for no reason at all, it seemed that everyone in Harlem had decided that *Macbeth* was the great triumph of their lives. The theater seated eleven, twelve hundred people. There were ten times that many milling about on Seventh Avenue. All the great Broadway swells got to rub elbows with Harlem pimps and numbers runners. When the play ended, there were so many curtain calls that I finally ordered it to be left open. So, the audience came up on stage to congratulate the actors. *(Still moved by this memory.)* That was magical. The critics, on the whole, were very kind to us… except our Mr. Hearst's man, Percy Hammond. I don't mean to speak ill of the dead, but his review… Negroes, he said, should never be seen in anything but plays about Negro life. You can imagine how that notion was received in Harlem. I was approached by one of our voodoo drummers, Abdul. We had imported Abdul and his troupe from the Gold Coast in Africa. *(Imitating an African witch-doctor.)* 'This critic bad man?' Sounds like an old Tarzan movie, doesn't it? I allowed as how he was. 'You want me make beri-beri on this bad man?' I told Abdul he was free to make all the beri-beri he wanted. 'We start devil drums now.' 'Go right ahead,' I answered, 'just be ready for tonight's performance.' 'Drums start now. Bad man die tomorrow.' And, in fact, the drumming that night was even more frenzied than usual. I didn't think anything more of it, until two days later when I learned that Mr. Percy Hammond had been found dead in his apartment. Now, I realise, on reflection this story may be hard to believe. But it's circumstantially true, nonetheless. *(Very ominously.)* And those critics with an axe to grind would do well to heed its meaning. *(Sitting down again; smiling.)* I'd only signed on for the one show; and now that it was up and running, I considered myself free of the WPA *and* John Houseman. But that wasn't to be, not until I came out here, anyway. *(Angrily.)* It was Houseman, you know, who started the rumor that I didn't write a word of *Citizen Kane*, that I only added my name to it as co-author. The truth is, I'd been carrying the idea of that script around with me for years – long before I'd ever heard the name, John Houseman. That summer I ran off to Ireland, I was in New York, waiting for the boat. And I went to see a play about a famous poet, Alison, and she's just died. Her friends and family are visited by a reporter who's there to do a story about the *real* Alison. All the world knows her work. But who was the person behind it? That's what he's there to find out. *(A devilish smile.)* The play went on to win the Pulitzer Prize. And ten years later, I made *Citizen Kane.* And not a single one of my... *(With absolute contempt.)* 'learned bee-ographers' has *ever* made the connection. *(Shaking his head in disbelief.)* No... they'd rather do like that Pauline Kael bitch and listen to Houseman discredit me.

WELLES' VOICE: *(Resigned to it.)* I fear the history of my glorious exploits may be the work of my enemies, who will mingle a thousand lies with a single grain of truth.

We hear the sound of a tape being rewound.

WELLES ON TAPE: It was Houseman, you know, who started the rumor that I didn't write a single word of *Citizen Kane,* that I only added my name to it.

WELLES sits there, stunned. A long pause.

WELLES: *(Exploding.)* You bastard! I bare my soul to you –

MEL'S VOICE: It's not what you're thinkin' –

WELLES: And for what? So you can run off bootleg copies for your professor to market?

MEL'S VOICE: I swear ta god, it's not like that!

WELLES: No? Then, what is it?

MEL'S VOICE: I didn't know how else to get your attention. Your Japanese are due here at three, an' we gotta make us some grocery money before then – so I can eat too. *(Pauses; cautiously.)* Okay?

WELLES: *(Quietly.)* Do you believe that story? *(No response.)* Do you?

MEL'S VOICE: *(Sincerely.)* Nobody that's ever seen *Chimes...* or *Touch of Evil...* even that crummy print of *Quixote* could listen to that shit.

WELLES: You can't imagine the harm it caused me. I've made so many fewer movies than I've wanted to because of it. I'd be doing my dancing bear routine, and my pigeon would ask... *(Mockingly.)* 'Is it true what I read about *Citizen Kane*?' I knew the minute that question came up I'd be going home empty-handed. Along with that other lie about my pictures never making any money –

MEL'S VOICE: That's what my professor told us.

WELLES: *(Flaring up again.)* Now you know why I despise academics. Miserable backstabbing peacocks, that's all they are! Shaw got it right: 'Those who can, do; those who can't, teach.' And the mumbo-jumbo they feed young people like yourself!!! There's some crackpot back East who would have you believe that my work is best understood through, and I quote, 'Bakhtin's formulation of the dialogic,' unquote.

MEL'S VOICE: What the hell does that mean?

WELLES: I should know? You'll have to ask that idiot professor of yours. And while you're at it, tell him to do his homework. Every one of my pictures has made money. Not immediately, perhaps. And certainly not the kind of box office that foolishness like *E.T.* and *Star Wars* have taken in. But they *have* made money. Are you recording this?

MEL'S VOICE: *(Weakly.)* Yes...

WELLES: Good! I want you to. It's about time *my* side of the story was heard. But you have to promise me you won't market what I'm telling you till after I'm gone.

MEL'S VOICE: Gone, as in.....?

WELLES: As in dead! *Muerto! Fini!* Then, how they'll miss me! Tears of mourning will be shed. Glycerin, of course – cleverly applied to look like the real thing on camera. I'll be 'rediscovered' – by the same miserable creatures who've savaged me in this life. *(Grunting cynically.)* It never fails.

MEL'S VOICE: Oh, c'mon!

WELLES: Don't believe me? Look at how Griffith was treated. We are all his children; he created our entire vocabulary. But in this town, there's no such thing as respect for one's elders. *(Puffs on his cigar.)* The children are much too busy trying to screw them out of their parking spaces. *(A pause.)* Have you ever listened to my *War of the Worlds* broadcast?

MEL'S VOICE: Every Halloween! Me an' the brothers –

WELLES: And I take it you've been to see *The Empire Strikes Back.*

MEL'S VOICE: Who hasn't?

WELLES: Those walking machines the enemy uses –

MEL'S VOICE: They were really cool!

WELLES: Do you remember how my Martians cross the Hudson River?

MEL'S VOICE: Sure! They had these machines with… legs that… *(Making the connection.)*… walked across! Whoa!!!

WELLES: A coincidence?

MEL'S VOICE: Makes you wonder!

WELLES: *(Picking up the phone.)* You *did* say three o'clock?

MEL'S VOICE: For what?

WELLES: *(Dialing.)* My Japanese.

MEL'S VOICE: Three o'clock.

WELLES: *(On the phone; expansively.)* Patrick! *(Listens.)* Fine, thank you. When can you have my table ready? *(Listens.)* Time enough to stop by the house and freshen up.

MEL enters hurriedly.

MEL: *(Upset.)* You're goin' where?

WELLES: *(On the phone.)* Prince Alessandro will be joining me for lunch.

MEL: Aren't you forgettin' –

WELLES: One moment, Patrick. *(To MEL; darkly.)* Forgetting what?

MEL: We got a shit-load of work ta do!

WELLES: Don't you think I know that?

No response.

Well?

MEL: *(Disgusted.)* Right! *(Exits.)*

WELLES: *(On the phone.)* Patrick? *(Listens; relieved.)* I was afraid I'd lost you. *(Listens.)* Actually, I thought I'd put my diet on hold for the day. So, what say we begin with a dozen sherried oysters... a good paté... half a wheel of runesten... and a bottle of pouilly-fume. *(Listens.)* All right then, the musigny blanc. The grilled tuna niçoise for me – unsalted, of course – and a tournedos steak for Alex. We'll wash it all down with a good beaujolais, and a pot of your blackest coffee. I don't imagine either of us will have any room left for dessert, but... *(Listens.)* No, the one before that, the mousse... *(Listening eagerly.)* Oui, à l'Armagnac! *(Listens.)* Who wouldn't be tempted? *(Listens.)* Yes, that's what I was going to suggest – but only a dollop or two.

As he listens, he puts on his glasses and idly flips through the pages of the notebook, until he comes to a particular piece of copy.

Where did you hear about *Quixote*? *(Listens; surprised.)* Really? I thought the trades had lost interest in my activities. Perhaps reaching seventy was deemed worthy of a line or two. *(Sarcastically; to himself.)* Or did they get wind of the company I was 'privileged' to keep last night? *(Listens.)* What is it? *(Listens.)* Oh yes, she was there, showing off her latest... enhancements. Being as it was my birthday, I was invited to be the first man allowed to touch them. Tell me, Patrick: however did we manage to survive as an industry before silicone implants? *(Gossiping.)* You know who else showed up? David Lean. *(Listens.)* That was his excuse. But who flies all the way from London to LA for beer and pretzels? *(Listens.)* Of course! He and Bob Bolt have a new project, *Nostromo*, and David was really there to hustle Spielberg. *(Listens.)* Not to worry, Patrick, I've already seen to that. Alex is over there pocketing the money, even as we speak.

MEL enters, carrying a music stand. He sets it down, then repositions the pole mike to hang in front of it.

I'd like you to hear this, Patrick, before I let you go. *(Dripping contempt as he reads.)* 'Just one new Baggies extra-protection freezer bag double-bags the freshness.' They think they're being so clever with their bag-this and bag-that. *(Listens; nodding.)* Spoken like a true friend. *(Listens.)* Yes. Yes, I'll see you in a bit. *(Hangs up; gives out a great sigh.)* Can we please get this over with?

MEL: Whadda ya say we try it standin' up?

WELLES: *(Obliging.)* Standing up, sitting down – it's still something for a backward child of five to read, not an actor.

MEL ignores his carping as he sets to the notebook on the music stand and adjusts the mike for WELLES, then exits.

MEL'S VOICE: Wanna gimme a level?

WELLES: *(Into the mike.)* I remain, obediently yours, Orson Welles.

MEL'S VOICE: *(Impressed.)* Where'd you come up with that?

WELLES: *(Pleased.)* It was my signature tag on the radio… once upon a distant time.

MEL'S VOICE: Cool!

WELLES: *(Looking into the booth.)* Now, can we please… get this…

He sees something that darkens his mood.

WELLES: Is there someone in the booth with you?

No response.

Mel? *(Steely; imperious.)* I'm talking to you. Is there someone in there with you?

No response.

I want you in here – NOW!!!

MEL enters.

Who's in there with you?

MEL: *(Evenly.)* The backward child of five that thought up that piece of copy.

WELLES: *(Bristling.)* I'm not used to having more than one person in there. *(Wandering off-mike as he points to the 'other person'.)* Not a word out of you – understood? I take direction from one person – under protest. But for two, I don't sit still.

MEL: Damn!!!

WELLES: *(Taken by surprise.)* What?

MEL: *(Exasperated.)* You're over there; the mike's over here.

WELLES: *(Realising.)* Ohhh!

He takes his place at the music stand, as MEL pretends to be put-out at having to re-adjust the microphone.

MEL: *(Stepping back.)* Say something.

WELLES: *(To the 'other person'; growling angrily.)* 'Baggies... new Baggies... doggie Baggies... garbage Baggies...'

MEL: *(Exiting.)* Okay, let's do it.

MEL'S VOICE: New Baggies... take one.

WELLES: 'Just one new Baggies... extra-protection... freezer bag... double-ba... *(Stumbles.)*... Shit!

MEL'S VOICE: Take two.

WELLES: 'Just one new Baggies extra-protection... freezer bag... double-bags... the freshness. Baggies unique formula of nylon... plus plastic... equals... the freshness protection... you'd get... by doubling up an ordinary bag.'

MEL'S VOICE: This time, could you play up –

WELLES: What do you mean, *this* time? I just did it correctly.

MEL'S VOICE: That was okay, but –

WELLES: Then, why are you asking me for another one? Why can't those machines of yours do the rest?

MEL'S VOICE: All we're askin' is a backup... just in case.

WELLES: We? I told you, I don't take direction from more than one person.

MEL'S VOICE: I meant me. New Baggies. Take three.

WELLES: *(Takes a sip of tea; clears his voice.)* 'Just one new Baggies... extra-protection freezer bag... double-bags the freshness. Baggies' unique formula... of nylon, plus plastic... equals the freshness protection you'd get by doubling up an ordinary bag.'

MEL'S VOICE: *(Upbeat.)* That's a keeper!

WELLES: *(Dripping sarcasm.)* Is it now? I couldn't be happier. Okay, what's next?

MEL'S VOICE: Citrocel.

WELLES: *(Turns the page; reading to himself.)* 'In the world of bulk laxatives, there's always been one problem... sandy, gritty taste. Now, there's one great-tasting oasis in this desert of grit... new clinically tested Citrocel...' *(To MEL.)* This is a very wearying one.

MEL'S VOICE: How so?

WELLES: It's full of things that are tough on the ear... to say nothing of unpleasant to read.

MEL'S VOICE: You did a dozen of them last year, and the best readin' –

WELLES: Was the one I gave then, and the one I'll give now.

MEL'S VOICE: Citrocel. Take one.

WELLES: 'In the world of bulk laxatives... there's always been one problem... sandy, gritty taste. Now, there's one great tasting oasis... new clinically tested Citrocel. Citrocel has the gentle action... doctors recommend. And every heaping teaspoon... is packed... with the fiber you need to promote... regularity. But when Citrocel hits cold water...' Do you see what I mean about this being tough on the ear? 'When Citrocel hits cold water... it bursts into a great-tasting orange liquid... you'll actually enjoy taking...' In a pig's ass you will! 'New Citrocel! The grit is gone!' *(Taking off his glasses.)* And so am I.

MEL'S VOICE: Not so fast!!!

WELLES: Now what?

MEL'S VOICE: There's still that job for the Brits.

WELLES: Can't it wait till after lunch?

MEL'S VOICE: I'm gonna need that time to work my Mello Magic and get it on the plane to London.

WELLES: Here, under protest, is Mrs. Buckley and her goddammed can of peas. *(Reading.)* 'We know a remote farm in Lincolnshire… where Mrs. Buckley lives. In July…' *(To MEL.)* What's the video like that goes with this copy?

No response.

Well?

MEL'S VOICE: I'm tryin' to find out for you. *(A pause.)* We open on this field. There's still snow on the ground.

WELLES: In July?

MEL'S VOICE: You know what I know. *(Pause.)* Okay… we see these plants comin' up.

WELLES: Mrs. Buckley's peas?

MEL'S VOICE: You got it!

WELLES: Why don't I say 'in July' *over* the snow? Isn't that the fun of it?

MEL'S VOICE: Done deal! But start a half-second later, when all that shit disappears.

WELLES: I think it's so nice to see a snow-covered field, then be told in July peas grow there. *(Returning to the copy.)* 'We know a remote farm… in Lincolnshire. In July… peas grow there…' *(To MEL.)* We're not even in the fields, you see, and she's already picked them. *(Thinks he hears something.)* What is it?

MEL'S VOICE: You know… pickin' in July.

WELLES: I don't understand you. What must be over in July?

MEL'S VOICE: *(Exasperated.)* When we get outta that fuckin' field!!!

WELLES: I *was* out. We were on to a big dish of peas, when I said, 'In July...'

MEL'S VOICE: Right! Can you play up the word in – '*in* July?'

WELLES: That doesn't make any sense. There's no known way of saying an English sentence in which you begin with 'in' and emphasize it. Get me a jury, show me where you can say '*in* July'... and I'll go down on you. '*In* July!' Impossible! Meaningless!

MEL'S VOICE: Then make it '*every* July.'

WELLES: '*Every* July?' But that's bad copy. Of course it's 'every July.' C'mon fellas, you're losing your heads. I wouldn't direct any living actor in Shakespeare like this. *(Takes off his glasses.)* Impossible! *(Ripping the copy from the notebook.)* You people take up more of my time than any other client I've ever had. That's right – you! I'm talking to you, the backward child of five. *(Brandishing the copy.)* I've been elevating shit like this all my life! ALL MY LIFE!!! Are you expecting me to be your stepping stone to another *E.T.?* Puerile shit like this to purity in peril – are those your horizons? Then, you should meet the master. I'll even provide you with a letter of introduction. *(As if reading from it.)* 'Dear Steven. Please welcome yet another recruit to your long green banner. You will find in him a true kindred spirit, whose Holy Grail, like yours, is billions at the box office.

MEL drowns out his tirade by playing 'The Charlie Kane Song' from Citizen Kane. *WELLES tries shouting over it. MEL responds by increasing the volume level.*

Bestow on him your papal blessing... of...'

Recognizing these inane lyrics, and how well they reflect the pointlessness of his current tirade, WELLES' mood changes, to one of uproarious laughter. Blackout.

*IF PERFORMED AS A LONG ONE-ACT, WITHOUT
AN INTERMISSION, THEN THE FOLLOWING
DON QUIXOTE QUOTE CAN BE USED AS
BLACKOUT BRIDGE, DURING WHICH THE SET
IS DIRTIED, WELLES CHANGES HIS COSTUME,
ETC. BUT ONE-ACT OR TWO, THE QUOTE
SHOULD BE HEARD BEFORE THE LIGHTS
COME UP FOR WELLES' ENTRANCE.*

WELLES' VOICE: A knight must roam the earth in
search of adventure so that his fame will have
preceded him when he arrives at the court of even
the greatest monarch. He must be so well known that
all the young lads will follow behind him through
the gates of the kingdom, shouting, 'Hail, Knight of
the Sun!' And recognizing this famous knight by his
armor, the sovereign will command his minions to go
forth and welcome this flower of chivalry that he may
sup with them.

*Lights up on the recording studio. It is strewn with empty
containers of Chinese take-out. Both phone lines are blinking
to show that people are on hold. WELLES enters, wearing a
navy blue suit and shirt, with a polka dot ascot. He is already
upset; all of the clutter infuriates him.*

WELLES: What's all this?

MEL'S VOICE: Say again?

WELLES: Get in here.

WELLES' VOICE: Whoever you may be, I pray that
I may not perish in this prison before my work is
ended.

MEL enters.

MEL: The Mello Man, at your service!

WELLES: *(Pointing.)* This mess you've made.

MEL reaches for the waste basket; but before he can clean up, WELLES sends the containers flying with a swing of his cane.

WELLES: *(Sitting down.)* Don't you know enough to pick up after yourself?

MEL: I didn't expect you back so soon.

WELLES: *(Reaching for the phone.)* I need an outside line.

MEL: They're all tied up.

WELLES: Well, *un*tie them!

MEL: There's a professor from USC on one –

WELLES: How many times do I have to tell you, I don't talk to their kind –

MEL: An' some dude from 'Sight n' Sound' on the other.

WELLES: That rag again?

MEL: He's got a question 'bout my all-time favourite flick.

WELLES: Does he now!

He picks up the phone and punches a number, as MEL exits.

This is Orson Welles. And you are? *(Listens.)* I don't talk to academics. Didn't … *(Interrupted.)* Didn't Houseman leave his papers to USC? All the more reason. *(Punching the other button.)* This is Orson Welles. I understand… *(Listens impatiently.)* I understand you want to take a little stroll down memory lane. Fuck memory lane! That's the past. I live in the present. Ask me what I'm doing today. *(Listens.)* Well…?

He cuts off his caller by punching the other number and dialing a number, his impatience rising as he waits.

WELLES' VOICE: Here I remain, Sancho, until you return with that letter. If the answer is as I hope, my penance will end.

WELLES: *(On the phone; anxiously.)* Alex? *(Waits.)* Shit! Dammit, man, where are you? I waited the better part of an hour for you to show up at The Saloon. It's about two. I'm back at work. Call me the minute you get this message.

He presses the other button, thumbs through his appointment book, finds a number and dials.

WELLES: *(At his most charming.)* Orson Welles for Steven Spielberg, please. *(Waits.)* Hello? To whom am I speaking? Vashti? And what, may I ask, is it you do for Steven? *(Listens.)* Assist his executive assistant. *(Reciting.)* 'I danced with the man who danced with the girl who danced with the Prince of Wales.' What is it? *(Listens.)* Just an old show tune, is all. You have to be a white-bearded old coot like me to remember it. I wonder, Vashti, if Steven could come to the phone. I promise not to take up too much of his... time... *(Listens.)* And his executive assistant, is she... *(Listens.)* I didn't realise the picture was in any shape to be screened. I meant to ask him at last night's doings, but... *(Listens.)* I only know what Oprah told me. She's predicting best picture, best director – best everything! Tell me, Vashti. I sent my man around this morning. *(Listens.)* Oh, you did? When he didn't show up for lunch... *(Listens.)* I'm sure he will, too. I can't today, but if Steven would like me to attend a screening... *(Listens.)* Not at all. He and Amy are two of my favourite people. How could I *not* want to help? *(Listens.)* Just have him give me a call, and I'll

be right over. Well... don't let me keep you. *(Listens.)*
Nice talking to you too, Vashti. And be sure to give
my love to Steve and Amy.

*Slowly, he hangs up, disgusted with himself at having to speak,
not with Spielberg, but with some faceless underling. MEL
enters to move the pole mike into position.*

MEL: You wanna sit or stand? *(Sizing up the situation.)*
I think you better stay put. *(Adjusting the mike.)* This
good for you?

WELLES: *(Absently.)* Yes... fine...

*He turns to face the mike. MEL makes a final adjustment,
then exits.*

MEL'S VOICE: The copy should be right on top.

WELLES puts on his glasses and opens the notebook.

MEL'S VOICE: I could do with a level.

WELLES: *(Reading.)* 'They come to us... because
their dreams... reach... far beyond... middle
management.'

MEL'S VOICE: Gotcha! Johnson an' Wales. Take one.

WELLES: 'They come to us... because their dreams...
reach... far beyond... middle management... or
because... their dreams... have changed over the
years. They come to us... because they're willing
to work... a little harder... to earn... a degree of
distinction. Whatever your interest... the Alan
Shawn Fein-steen Graduate School... at Johnson and
Wales... University... has a masters... or doctoral
program... that matches... your dream of a better
life. Johnson and Wales... distinction... by degrees.'

MEL'S VOICE: I need you to say the name again. It's
Fein-stein, not Fein-steen.

WELLES: The Alan Shawn Fein-steen Graduate School at –

MEL'S VOICE: Again!

WELLES: The Alan Shawn Fein-steen… shit!

The phone begins ringing, creating even more distraction for him.

MEL'S VOICE: Whadda ya drink beer from?

WELLES: I don't drink beer.

MEL'S VOICE: *(Snapping.)* If you did!

WELLES: A stein?

MEL'S VOICE: Gimme three in a row, just like that.

WELLES: *(With varying inflections.)* A stein… a stein… a stein.

MEL'S VOICE: *(Satisfied.)* Magic time!!!

WELLES: *(Finally.)* How long do you intend to let it ring?

MEL'S VOICE: It's probably for you.

WELLES: And what if it is?

MEL'S VOICE: *(Frustrated.)* Hey, man, I'm tryin' ta make us some Mello Magic in here, ya know!

WELLES: Answer the damned thing!

MEL'S VOICE: *(Pauses.)* Do you know a cop name of Shore… or Shull? I can't tell which from this guy's accent.

WELLES: Am I supposed to?

MEL'S VOICE: You sent his ass to jail. Anyway, he's just died, an' his hometown paper's on the line. They wanna know if you'd like ta make a statement.

WELLES: *(Rising.)* I hope he rots in hell.

MEL'S VOICE: A southern sheriff goin' ta jail for beatin' up a black man! That's gotta be a first.

WELLES: He didn't just beat him up; he gouged his eyes out.

(He comes downstage to a 1940s standing microphone and takes out a legal document.)

WELLES: Good morning. This is Orson Welles speaking. I'd like to read to you from an affidavit. 'I, Sergeant Isaac Woodard, Jr., being duly sworn, do depose and state as follows: I am 27 years old and a veteran of the United States Army, having served for 15 months in the South Pacific and earned one battle star. I was honorably discharged on February 12th, 1946 from Camp Gordon, Georgia. While still in uniform, I bought a bus ticket to Winslow, South Carolina to get my wife so we could go on up to New York and visit my father and mother. About an hour out of Augusta, the driver stopped at a small drugstore. I asked if there was time for me to go to the restroom. He cursed me and said no. When he cursed me, I cursed him back. When the bus reached Batesburg, he went and got the police. They didn't give me a chance to explain. The policeman struck me with his billy and told me to shut up. He asked if I was discharged. When I said yes, he started beating me with his billy across the top of my head. When I came to, he was poking me in the eyes with the end of his billy. Then, he threw me in a cell and locked me up. I woke up the next morning... and couldn't see. He said, 'C'mon, nigger, me and you are going to hear what the judge has to say.' I told him I could not see to come out of my cell… I was blind. He said, 'Feel your way out!' He said I'd be all right after I washed my face. He led me up to the judge. After I told the judge what happened, he said, 'We don't have those kind of goings-on here in Batesburg. I fine you fifty dollars, or thirty days in jail.'

WELLES' VOICE: *(With quiet resolve.)* This prompts me to do that for which I was sent into the world, and to which end I vowed at all times to aid those who are oppressed.

WELLES: *(Setting aside the affidavit.)* Now, it seems the officer of the law who blinded the young Negro has not been named. The boy saw him while he still had eyes, but he had no way of knowing which particular policeman it was who brought the justice of Dachau and Auschwitz to Batesburg, South Carolina. He was just another white man with a club who wanted to show a Negro where he belonged – in the darkness. Until we know more about him, we'll call this policeman Officer X. He might be listening to this broadcast. I hope so. Officer X, I'm speaking to you. Enjoy your anonymity, Officer X… while it lasts… because you're going to be uncovered. The whole world is going to know your given name – and, yes, your so – called Christian name. Assume another one, and I will make sure the name you would forget is not forgotten. I will remove from you all refuge. And after I've found you out, I'll never lose you, Officer X. If they try you, I plan to watch the trial. If they jail you, I'll be at the prison gates for your first day of freedom. I want to see for myself the kind of human being who will admit to knowing you, Officer X. You can't get rid of me. What business is this of mine, you ask? God help me if this isn't the most pressing business I have. That soldier you saw fit to blind fought for me in the war. You too, probably. The least I can do now is fight for him. So, I come to this microphone in his name, and in the name of all those who have no voice of their own. We want to know where stands the sun of common fellowship? When will it finally rise over Batesburg, South Carolina? Your fate, Officer X, will tell the rest of us where we are going with our American experiment – into bankruptcy, or into that serene tomorrow with freedom and justice, for all the Negro soldier hoped for when he had eyes and, with eyes open, went to war. *(Pauses; then, very soft-spoken.)* Now, I see it's time for me to say goodbye. Please let me call again… same time next Sunday. Until then, I remain… as always… obediently yours.

MALE ANNOUNCER: *(Very mannered.)* And now the words we always use on these broadcasts: Mr. Welles' opinions are his own and do not reflect the views of ABC or our sponsor, Lear Radio.

Amused by this disclaimer, WELLES lights his cigar and takes a puff.

WELLES: That they didn't! I received more hate mail for the Woodard broadcasts than anything I'd done before, or since – including *War of the Worlds*. The good citizens of Batesburg went so far as to burn me in effigy. *The Stranger* was scheduled to play for a few days in Batesburg, but the city fathers saw fit to ban it – along with any other pictures I might make in the future. *(Amused.)* Not that I'm unaccustomed to being banned. For thirty years, the mere mention of my name was forbidden by our Mr. Hearst to all his subject newspapers. But to be banned by an entire city – an *American* city, no less – that was quite something! The end result of the *War of the Worlds* scandal was to earn me a sponsor, Campbell's Soup.

Isaac Woodard ended my career in radio. A boycott of Lear products was threatened by some race-baiting preacher in Mississippi. Stations – north as well as south – threatened to break away from the full network, if they didn't take that 'nigger lover' *(Indicating himself.)* off the air. 1946! I was the ripe old age of thirty-one. No longer the Boy Wonder. No, I had a new distinction: world's youngest has-been. *(Smiling.)* I've said it before and I'll say it again: I started at the top… and have been working my way down ever since. Ireland, New York, Chicago –

MEL'S VOICE: We gotta lay down those testimonials before your Japanese get here.

WELLES: I didn't know what it meant to fail until I came out here to Hollywood. Door after door slammed on me. RKO pulled one of those South American things – you know, where the colonels come in the night to overthrow you.

MEL'S VOICE: *(Very insistent.)* Hello in there!!!

WELLES: I heard you the first time. *(To the audience.)* The morning after I was ordered off the lot, they hung a banner over the main gate: 'ALL'S WELL THAT ENDS WELLES!' *(Sitting down again.)* What testimonials?

 MEL'S VOICE: That phone company in Delaware.

WELLES: *(Locating the copy.)* Delaware Wireless?

MEL'S VOICE: You got it!

WELLES: *(Reading to himself.)* 'When it comes to cellular, what's most important to a Delaware Wireless customer?' *(To MEL.)* The word wireless reminds us of Marconi, but we're supposed to believe they're state-of-the-art. Does that make sense to you?

MEL'S VOICE: *(Coldly.)* They pay their bills on time; *that* makes sense to me. Delaware Wireless. Take one.

WELLES: *(Clears his throat.)* 'When it comes to cellular… what matters most… to a Delaware… Wireless… customer…'

His enhanced voice continues as he gets up from his chair.

WELLES ON TAPE: For Suzie Potter of Wilmington Mutual, it's coverage. For Jerry Izzo of T.C.C.A., it's affordability. And for John Kole of Kole and Company, it's customer service.

WELLES: A lot of things came to an end in 1946, my marriage to Rita among them. We were known around town as Beauty and the Brain. Beauty replaced the Brain with the Bank Account, Aly Khan, and when that quickly soured, she took up with the Brute, Dick Haymes. The Alzheimer's took what little was left after he was done with her. *(Almost too painful to recall.)* The last time I saw Rita was at The Saloon. I was having dinner, and she was seated at one of the other tables. Naturally, I went over to say hello. When I kissed her on the cheek… my blood ran cold. She didn't even recognize me. 'Death lay on her like an untimely frost / Upon the sweetest flower in all the field.' *(Pausing to collect himself.)* I was shooting a movie in Brazil, and… well, I'm one of those people who's always looking for something to read. The only thing I could get my hands on were back issues of *Life* magazine. And there on the cover was Rita. You know the picture: she's in a slip, kneeling on a bed, looking over her shoulder at the camera. Every GI in World War Two carried it with him.

WELLES' VOICE: *(Lovestruck.)* Her locks are scarlet; her cheeks, roses; her eyes, suns; her smiles, rainbows. As for those parts that modesty keeps covered, they are not to be compared to any other.

WELLES: I stared at that picture and said to myself, I'm going to marry that girl. Hedda the Hat got wind of my intentions and wrote it up in her column. Rita was furious. She thought I was amusing myself at her expense. She had no self-esteem, you see. That whole Love Goddess image that Harry Cohn thought up for her had nothing to do with Rita Hayworth. She never got a moment's pleasure out of being a movie star. 'The minute I have a flop', she'd say, 'I'll be nobody again.' When we finally met, I said, 'The papers say I want to marry you. Guess what? It's true.' She turned on her heel and walked away. *(Pleased with himself.)* Well… I go the distance in the chase. I'll wait under your window till four in the morning, if I have to. *(Savouring the memory.)* I once paid a man a hundred dollars to go up in a plane and write the seven of hearts in the skies over Central Park. I was on the ground with the ballerina I was courting. 'Take a card', I said, '*any* card.' Of course, she took the card I wanted her to, the seven of hearts. 'Would you like to find it in your purse?' I asked. 'No? In my pocket? Or written in the sky?' 'Written in the sky!' she said. So, I pointed, a la Houdini; and sure enough, there in the skies over New York City was the seven of hearts. I was that kind of romantic fellow. It took me six weeks to get Rita to answer the phone; but when she did, we went out that very evening. Six weeks after that, we tied the knot, as they say. No-one was supposed to know, least of all Harry Cohn, who was as adamant that we *not* marry as he was against my sawing her in half for the Mercury Wonder Show. But this time, there was no stopping us. So, Harry milked our wedding for all the publicity he could wring out of it. They were all waiting for us, all the gossips... except Louella Parsons. She wrote for the Hearst syndicate and, because, Rita was aligning herself with the enemy... *(Indicating himself.)*... Louella stopped writing about her. It's hard to believe the influence they had. Winchell. Louella. Hedda the Hat. Dorothy Kilgallen. They ruined more people in this town than HUAC. *(Pausing.)* I've always believed that Harry Cohn was behind my break-up with Rita. The truth is, he wanted her for himself. Rita's whole life had been one of doing as she was told. Except... she flatly refused to sleep with Harry. So, if he couldn't possess her physically, he would make her dependent on him in every *other* way. And in that he succeeded... until I came along. Rita was supposed to marry Victor Mature, the reigning hunk of his day. *(Imitating Cohn.)* 'Hollywood wants that marriage!' But as I would learn, you crossed Harry Cohn at your peril. Rita had no formal education. Her father's doing. He made her his dancing partner at the age of twelve. And Rita was painfully aware of it. If we had guests over, she'd just sit there and say nothing. If we went anywhere – a friend's house, a rally for the president – she'd say, 'People are staring at me. They think I'm stupid.' No amount of reassuring on my part could change her mind. Harry approached the problem of Rita's insecurities another way. *(Imitating Cohn.)* 'You're a dancer', he'd tell her. 'You're not supposed to think.' *(Normal again.)* And he made sure to surround her with studio functionaries – script girls, hairdressers, that sort. Of course, they were all his spies and filled her head with stories about my being unfaithful. I'd come home to find her in tears. 'I know all about you and...so-and-so', she'd say. There was nobody else, not at that point in our relationship. So, Harry coiled himself up in a corner and waited

for me to make a mistake. Cole Porter called from
New York. He wanted to know if I'd like to direct a
musical he'd written, *Around the World in 80 Days*. I'd
done it on radio. And the thought of being back on
Broadway – who can resist that? Theater's not a high
priority here in Tinseltown. You can't make a living
in the theater. I never did, not even when Houseman
and I were running those theaters in New York, the
Mercury and the WPA. If it hadn't been for my radio
earnings, we could never have made ends meet, even
with Uncle Sam as our angel. Mr. Roosevelt, once
said I was the only private citizen he ever knew who
put money *into* a government project. I didn't know it
then, but that set a pattern for the rest of my life. If
there was something I *really* wanted to do, and I
couldn't find backing for it, I'd put up my own
money. Anyway… Cole had written this musical.
'Don't touch it,' I was warned. 'Cole Porter's all
written out.' *(Laughs ironically.)* Written out, was he?
Cole's next show was *Kiss Me Kate*. Mike Todd was
our producer. I remember thinking, 'This is a man
who can sell anything,' little knowing that Cole and I
were next in line – to be sold out! We were in Boston
for the first tryout, when Mike announced he was
quitting the show. Mind you: this was the same Mike
Todd who would later make millions off the movie. If
I'd had any sense, I'd have closed the show right then
and there. Instead, I called the cast around me, like
in one of those old movie musicals, and said, 'Kids!
We're going to put this show on, come hell or high
water!' By the time we made it to Broadway I had
something like $400,000 of my own money in it. Of
course, none of this made any impression on the
critics, who dismissed it as an 'empty extravaganza.'
The other shoe fell at tax time. I had declared the
$400,000 as a business expense. But the IRS said,
'Oh no, you'll just have to take it as a personal loss.'

That show left me in debt to them for years to come. I forget whether we were still in Boston. Anyhow, I had to come up with $50,000 if we were to go on that evening. I checked with the box office to see what we had in the way of receipts, but they gave me the empty pockets sign. So, I said to myself, 'Who do I know that would give me $50,000 by 2p.m.?' Darryl Zanuck – of course! But he was traveling in Europe and couldn't be reached in time. *(Chagrined.)* So, I called Harry Cohn. He was all smiles on the phone, like the cat that was about to swallow the canary. In this case, *two* canaries. Rita's contract was up for renewal, and she was after him to cast her in something that would give her a chance to do some acting for a change. No doubt, he blamed me for putting that bug in her ear. *(Imitating Cohn.)* 'Who do you think you are, Bette Davis?' Or as the kids say nowadays, 'If it ain't broke, don't fix it.' So, Harry decided to teach her a lesson. And what better way than to cast her in a Welles picture? 'So, what do I get for my fifty grand?' he asked. *(Laughing.)* I could have pitched the Yellow Pages and he'd have okayed it. Of course, I didn't realise it at the time. At the time, I thought *I* was hustling *him.* Little did I know! I looked around the box office. One of the cashiers was reading a paperback. I grabbed it from her and said, 'I have in my hand the best book I've ever read. It's called…' I had to check to be sure… *If I Die Before I Wake.* (*As Cohn.*) 'What does Rita get to do in it?' As if he cared! 'The role of a lifetime,' I assured him. 'Her public's going to see a whole new Rita Hayworth.' Of course, that's what he was hoping, that she'd get in over her head – and blame me for it. Which is what happened. The money arrived at the appointed hour, and I found myself committed to making this expensive Hayworth 'A' picture from a novel I hadn't even read. When I finally got around to it, I thought, 'Dear god! This doesn't make the least bit of sense.' So, I wrote an entirely *new* story, and called it *The Lady from Shanghai*. The new Rita needed a new look. So, I cut off her glorious red hair, and dyed the rest platinum blond. You can imagine Harry's reaction. *(Cohn in a rage.)* 'What's that crazy bastard done this time?' No sooner was the rough cut ready than Harry insisted on a preview. This was the moment he'd been waiting for, and he played it to the hilt. The film ended. Lights went up. The room was so quiet you could have heard an option drop. Harry just sat there, his mouth open, staring at the screen. *(As Cohn.)* 'I'll give a thousand dollars to anyone who can explain this piece of shit to me!' *(Smiles; puffs on his cigar.)* Say what you will, the man had a way with words. I wasn't allowed to, and no-one else dared – explain the film to him, that is. Harry and his 'yes-men' formed a human shield around Rita – no doubt, to protect her against my evil influence – and, one by one, they got their licks in. The piece of shit in question was dismissed as artsy and obscure. That may be true of *Blood of the Poet*, but not *Lady from Shanghai*. Did I realise the harm I'd done to Rita's career? She only received her best reviews for that picture. Harry took her hand in his, and swore on his mother's grave that he'd move heaven and earth to make certain her star was never tarnished again. Of course, he'd make her eat crow in the bargain. She had to agree to *Lady* being released as a 'B' picture, which had tongues wagging around town. And to throw HUAC off the scent, Harry got Rita to denounce me for leading her astray politically. I was finished as far as Hollywood was concerned. Without Mr. Roosevelt's coat-tails to hide behind, and that pygmy who succeeded him furious with me for shaming his Attorney General into indicting the rogue cop who blinded Isaac Woodard, I suddenly found myself facing a Congressional subpoena – *and* being pursued by the IRS for back taxes. *(Sardonically.)* It was only after I'd forced his hand that our Mr. Truman became the great champion of civil rights that history regards him today. *(Puffs on his cigar.)* My father once took my brother, Dickie, and me aside and said, 'There are only two things it's ever seemly for a gentleman to be thinking: what did god intend by creating the universe, and what do I do next?' *(Relishing the memory.)* His only other words of wisdom were: 'Never drink port before champagne; and avoid making love to your wife in the morning, so you can be ready if something better shows up during the day.' *(Nods knowingly.)* For once, I did something sensible… I boarded a plane for Rome, and didn't return to this country for the better part of ten years.

MEL'S VOICE: I'm about ready for you.

WELLES: The silver lining in all this was, I got to make *Othello.* Of course, it took me four years, and only added to my reputation as a madman. I was raising money at a hundred thousand a clip. That was my fee in those days. I'd tell people: I'm a whore; I'll do anything for that hundred thousand – except direct. It took a lot of whoring to finish that picture. Cesare Borgia, Cagliostro – the dogs I let myself be cast in! Then, I'd dash off and shoot until my money ran out. That was the reason I moved *Othello* from Venice to Morocco – money. It went further in Morocco. Even so, I had to shoot everything in shot/reverse shot… because I could never get all of my actors in front of the camera at the same time. *(Sharing his secret with them.)* When you see anyone from behind, with a hood over his head, you can bet it's a stand-in.

Softly, the theme song for The Third Man *can be heard.*

WELLES' VOICE: You know what the fella said, 'In Italy, for thirty years under the Borgias, they had warfare, bloodshed, murder – and they produced Leonardo, Michelangelo and the Renaissance. In Switzerland, they had brotherly love and five hundred years of peace and democracy. And what did that produce? The cuckoo clock!'

WELLES: I don't often wish for the chance to do something over again. But that was certainly one of those times! I was offered a choice between my usual hundred thousand and a share of the profits. Mind you: this was before the days of creative accounting, when it was still possible for a movie to turn a profit. *(Music out.)* Nowadays, they can work the numbers so that even *E.T.* ends up in the red. In this country, *The Third Man* was only a success. But in Europe… well, there's never been such a hit over there. It's still playing in Vienna, all these many years later! *(Big laugh.)* I could have bank-rolled ten *Othellos*, if I'd opted to share in the profits! Since I was calling the shots, and there was no Harry Cohn to fire me, I was determined to make *exactly* the picture I wanted, a great luxury in this business, which I've enjoyed only one other time – with *Citizen Kane*. The obvious place to launch *Othello* should have been Venice, but the only print available at the time was woefully inadequate. So, I held out for Cannes. The smart money that year was on Elia Kazan for *Viva Zapata*. There was also some fellow from one of those minuscule city-states in the Balkans who the critics had anointed 'darling of the festival.' *(In disbelief.)* His home movie was being compared to the *best* of John Ford! *(Another shared secret.)* Want to know the key to success with that crowd? Make a movie about nothing. In a language no-one understands. With no story, lousy acting, and the worst possible photography. But here's the secret: subtitles. Add enough of them and the critics will outdo each other with praise. My *real* reason for being at Cannes wasn't to win anything; I just wanted to line up a distributor. I was in my room at the Carlton when I received a call asking me if I happened to know the Moroccan national anthem. Since so much of it had been shot there, I thought it only right that *Othello* be presented as the Moroccan entry. There was no official delegation or anything, just me and my cans of film. Can't say that I do, I told my caller. But I certainly understood why he was calling. That evening, as I mounted the stage to collect my Golden Palm, I couldn't help but laugh as the festival orchestra scratched out something vaguely Oriental, and the audience stood solemnly to attention. United Artists picked up the film, but didn't get around to distributing it for another three years. When they finally did, the critics promptly dismissed it as 'meretricious nonsense.' And I quote: 'To connoisseurs of Shakespeare, this film can only be torture.' Unquote. These same connoisseurs wouldn't dare criticize Verdi. And, god knows, his *Othello* is a far cry from Shakespeare. So why should my movie be more faithful than Verdi's opera? *(The phone rings.)* You can't just put a play on the screen – *any* play! Connoisseurs, my ass! *(Another ring.)* Mark my words: if Shakespeare were alive today, he'd be writing for movie-of-the-week.

MEL'S VOICE: It's his majesty on the phone for you.

WELLES: *(Suddenly alert.)* What is it?

MEL'S VOICE: Your flunkey, he's –

WELLES: *(Grabbing the phone.)* Alex! Where in god's name have you been? *(Listens.)* I know; I called over there. I had to sweet talk some twit who works for him. *(Listens.)* Yes, that's her. Vashti! What kind of name is Vashti? Our Steven goes in for all that… exotic… shit…

His voice trails off as he hears the truth. Dazed, he lowers himself into the chair.

What do you mean, 'overextended'? *(Listens.)* He gave absolutely no hint of it last night. So, what happened between then and now to overextend him? *(Listens.)* Well, well, well! Found someone new to fuck over, has he? I'm not sport enough for him anymore? *(Listens.)* And David believed him? After all these years, you'd think he'd know better. What am I saying? I've just had *my* bell rung, haven't I? You stay put; I'm going to call David.

He puts Tasca on hold, finds a number in his book, and dials.

MEL'S VOICE: *(Beside himself.)* Whadda ya think you're doin'?

WELLES ignores him. MEL charges into the studio.

MEL: It's after three, for chrissake!!!

WELLES: *(On the phone.)* It's Orson Welles for David Lean.

MEL: Do you hear what I'm sayin'?

WELLES: We'll get started when I'm damned good and ready.

MEL grabs a chair and sits backward on it, tapping his foot impatiently and glaring at WELLES.

WELLES: David? Orson. *(Listens.)* Not so good, I'm afraid. *(Glancing at MEL.)* You see, I have this knife sticking out of my back. And who do you think put it there? *(Listens.)* Believe it, David. *(Listens.)* He all but licked my balls last night. Yours too, as I recall. Now, I'm not worth chump change to him. *(Listens.)* What do you mean, he has a point? *(Listens.)* Don't go changing the subject on me, goddammit! I want to know what you meant by that remark. *(Listens.)* How would it be throwing good money after bad? *(Listens.)* If *Quixote* meant that much to me? Do you doubt it, David? *(Listens.)* Fuck him! Do *you* doubt it? *(Listens; sadly.)* Then, you deserve the screwing he has in store for you. *(Listens.)* Of course I'm bitter. A year from now, you'll be bitter, too. How much are you looking to get out of him for *Nostromo*? *(In disbelief.)* Mark my word: you'll never see a dime of that money – not next year, not the year after that, not ever. *(Another glance at MEL.)* David, please – don't make the same mistake I did. *(Listens; resigned.)* All right. But don't say I didn't warn you. *(Punching the other button.)* Alex? *(Listens.)* He's no more inclined to listen than I was. I wish I knew what to tell you… about where we go from here. *(Trying to make light of the situation.)* Looks like you've hitched your wagon to a *falling* star, old friend. All I know is… well… I have some very serious thinking to do. *(Listens.)* Yes, there may yet be another film out there. Miracles do happen, after all. I have to believe that. If I didn't, if I thought this… *(Ruffling the pages of voice-over copy.)*… was all I had to look forward to…

MEL: *(Something catches his eye.)* Speaking of which… *(He exits quickly.)*

WELLES: I appreciate the offer, but… *(Listens.)* No, I'll be just fine. Tell me, Alex, what's your weekend looking like? *(Listens.)* I need someone I can trust to strap on a money belt and make a run down to Panama for me. I have a few dollars I'd like deposited in my account down there.

MEL'S VOICE: Minus the three hundred thou you're about to blow off.

WELLES: *(Gesturing for MEL to be quiet.)* Away from the watchful eyes of the IRS and all.

MEL'S VOICE: Because your Japanese are about to walk the fuck outta here, if you don't get off that phone.

WELLES: I have to go. Think it over and call me at home later. *(Hangs up; explodes at MEL.)* Who the hell do you think you are, talking to me like that?

MEL'S VOICE: *(Just as angry.)* Who am I? Just the best goddammed friend you have. I can't get you another picture to direct, but I sure as hell can keep you in grocery money. I'm the guy who makes you sound like Orson Welles – remember? Without me, buddy, you're up shit's creek!!!

WELLES: You think so?

MEL'S VOICE: I *know* so. This is you.

We hear WELLES on tape, his painfully labored reading of the Laddy Boy spot.

This is me.

We hear the finished version of the same commercial, with WELLES' voice gloriously restored by MEL's machines.

MEL'S VOICE: You tell me who you'd put your money on.

WELLES just sits there, utterly vanquished.

WELLES' VOICE: I was born to be the target at which the arrows of misfortune are aimed.

MEL enters, visibly moved to see WELLES like this. A pause.

137

MEL: *(Quietly.)* Look… they're *my* Japanese too. And I wanna keep doin' business with them.

WELLES: *(Distantly.)* And that won't happen –

MEL: Not if you keep dickin' 'em around, it won't.

WELLES: *(Amused.)* Is that what I've been doing – dicking them around? *(His laughter building.)* Then, my young Houdini, henceforth I shall be dickless to a fault. You have my word on it!

MEL: *(Bewildered.)* Why don't I go get 'em?

WELLES: Yes, you do that. *(MEL starts off.)* But first, I need you to do me a favour.

MEL: Name it.

WELLES: Turn off that bootleg tape you've been making.

MEL: *(Smiling.)* I did that a long time ago.

WELLES: *(Unscrewing his thermos.)* And your promise?

MEL: Not till you're gone – scout's honour!

He exits as WELLES pours a cup of tea. After a sip, he reaches into his bag and takes out a book, thumbing through it until he finds the right page, which he folds back. Seeing MEL and the others in the booth, he rises politely.

MEL'S VOICE: Mr. Welles, this is Mr. Yamazaki.

WELLES: *(Very deferential.)* Yamazaki-san…

MEL'S VOICE: Mr. Ogawa.

WELLES: Ogawa-san…

MEL'S VOICE: And Mr. Iwamatsu.

WELLES: Gentlemen!

MEL'S VOICE: I see you already have something to read.

WELLES: Yes…

MEL'S VOICE: Then, what say we get started?

WELLES: I second that.

He sits down and takes another sip of tea.

MEL'S VOICE: Ready? *(WELLES nods.)* Tape's rollin'. Story number one. Take one.

WELLES: *(Reflectively.)* Isak Dinesen was a Dane, and I've been in love with her ever since I opened her first book. In life, she was the Baroness Blixen – Tania, to her close friends. I've known some of these friends, and have never stopped pumping them for every morsel of information, every memory of her, however slight. I wrote a letter to her once. When I was done, there was a perfect mountain of pages, every one of which I carefully destroyed. I boarded a plane to visit this person whom I loved, as Ben Jonson said of Shakespeare, this side idolatry. She was living then in the same house where she was born, and where she died. Hamlet's Elsinore is just up the road. She had been persuaded to let me call on her in the morning. I spent a sleepless night and, at daybreak, took the first plane out of Copenhagen. What could such a casual visitor have presumed to offer, except his stammered thanks? The visitor would have been a bore, and the lover was too proud for that. I had only to keep silent and our affair would last, on the most intimate terms, for as long as I had eyes to read.

He puts on his glasses and opens the book to the page he has marked.

WELLES: *The Dreamers* by Isak Dinesen.

He takes a deep breath and begins to read, his flawless delivery and legendary voice restored to him.

'What is life, when you think on it,' Lincoln Forsner asked, 'but a fiendishly complicated process for turning fat, playful puppies into blind, mangy dogs, and beamish young boys, for whom the world holds infinite promise, into broken old men with runny eyes?' 'What is man,' answered the Storyteller, 'but an ingenious machine for turning wine into urine? You might even ask which is the greater craving, to drink or to make water? But through it all, a poem has been written, a prophet begotten, a kiss stolen, a joke told.' 'And afterwards?' Lincoln Forsner asked. 'Afterwards, the world is pleased to piss us out again.' 'How, I'd like to know, are you able to put so good a face on something that only wants to rid itself of you?' 'I dream,' said the Storyteller. 'Dream?' 'Yes; by the grace of god, every night when I close my eyes. And in my dreams I see endless horizons, such as there are none in this life.' *(With the greatest of emotion.)* 'May god have mercy on me,' said Lincoln Forsner, 'for I no longer know... what it is... to dream.'

Slowly, WELLES closes the book and, removes his glasses.

WELLES' VOICE: When asked what the best death was, Julius Caesar answered, 'Quick, and without warning.' Even though Caesar spoke as a pagan, he was right.

Overjoyed, MEL rushes into the studio.

MEL: My man! You know what you just did? You nailed that sucker dead on! *(Pointing to the booth.)* Ain't a dry eye in there – an' they didn't understand a word you were sayin'! No two ways about it, baby – you still the man!!!

Obviously in a great hurry, MEL begins dismantling the equipment.

They wanna take you for a drink. The Saloon, Four Seasons – anyplace you want. Your Mello Man, he's got this little starletto with headlights out to here waitin' on him over Silver Lake way. Me an' her's gonna blaze us some haze. I don't hafta tell an ol' stick man like you where we goes from there.

WELLES smiles absently and begins to collect his things. His thoughts are clearly elsewhere. WELLES' movements are much too slow for MEL.

MEL: *(Losing patience with him.)* That's a wrap, dude! C'mon, up an' at 'em!

WELLES lights a cigar and slowly crosses to the door. Suddenly, he stops and turns to MEL, smiling wickedly.

WELLES: Remember what I said about being something of a magician?

MEL: *(Exploding.)* MR. WELLES!!!

WELLES points to the studio and snaps his fingers. Blackout.

The End.

JAMES DEAN IS DEAD!
(Long Live James Dean)

By Jackie Skarvellis

This version of *James Dean is Dead! (Long Live James Dean)* was first performed at Above the Stag Theatre with Stephen Cheriton as James Dean on 4th June 2009.

DEAN: Some crash huh? Whatta way to go, one helluva way to go! My Spyder Porsche, my baby. Oh, I never thought I'd die in her, not in the way I did! Steering wheel through my chest, broken ribs, broken neck, I was a mess. But, hey! That's show business! So, where shall I begin? Why not at the end? I'm in Limbo, living in my mind. Let me take you back in time, back to a time when I was a star…

You're the greatest, you're the best! Sexy beast, animal! That's me! Mad, bad, dangerous to know, that's Byron, famous English poet. Byron is my middle name – my Mom loved poetry. That's me! So a few guys get hurt, a few gals too. That's the name of the game. I'm good, I'm great, I charm the public, seduce the fans – thousands of them. It's easy, like taking candy from a baby! Razzle dazzle 'em, I'm hip, I'm slick. I'm nobody, I'm only as good as my next job, the next part I play. No role, no me, then I'm nobody. But give me that role and I'm on a roll! Brando's the best, worship that guy. But watch out, Marlon, cos I'm catching up quick! Look out, here comes Jimmy Dean! Love me in spades, nobody else does, just my fans and there's a lot of 'em.

Twenty four summers, young enough to feed the legend! Live fast, die young! I sure as shit lived fast! On the knife edge, the Knife of Life. It sticks you on it and twists you in the gut! It's my last day on Earth, I keep reliving it. Going to a race in Salinas, my death race. Rolf was sitting next to me, he lived, my mechanic lived. He'd checked her out real well, she was running like a dream, engine purring – like a big cat! My Spyder Porsche, feed my legend Baby! Hollywood Vultures! I was on the crest of a wave that day, on the up and up. In love with speed, speed, love it, always have been in love with it! Great stuff. Open the road up, wide open, like fucking some guy in his ass! Comfortable, wheel between my hands, I'm in control, power between my legs! We stop off at Tips Diner for a shake, some guy eyes me up and down – got no time, no time for anything except driving on and on into the silver-grey twilight. Car's silver too, hard to see in this light that's no light between worlds, the light between two worlds – between Life and Death. The Limbo light. I'm still in Limbo, still speeding, still in eternity. Going fast, faster still, as fast as I can: slam my foot down. There's something coming, something in the way, roadblock? No, another car coming straight for me. He's gotta see me, gotta stop! STOP! *(Car crash.)* Limbo! I'm in Limbo again! I'm reliving my life over and over again, it never ends! They won't let it end! They won't let me go – they'll never let me go!

Immortality, that's all that matters. That's all that counts in my book. How to live forever, to be immortal. If a man survives in people's minds after his death: that's real fame! And I got that now. From where I am I can see them standing there in lines, queuing up to do just what I done, the same thing: the Death Ride! My Death Ride! Long rows of 'em, a never-ending stream of kids: all clones of me, doing just what I done. They're even dressed the same: tight blue jeans, white t-shirt, red nylon zipper jacket, same haircut, same style, they walk like me, they even try to talk like me – to be me! They never even met me five decades ago, five decades since my death – more. All of 'em, imitating me! That is fame. I got it at last, but I had to die to get it! It feeds the legend, ya see: Live Fast, Die Young! Twenty-four summers: the stuff of legend. It's romantic. That's Immortality!

Bells toll.

Oh Momma, Momma! Why did you die and leave
me all alone? I was nine, nine years old! How did
you expect me to do it all alone? I can't do it on
my own! Where are you? I come here when I'm
feeling down and talk to her – talking to the dead. I
hold onto the cold stone: it's her body and it never
gets warm. I tell her how tough it's been, it's hard,
Momma, to do it. I hope she hears me, I hope she
understands. I do it all the time – talk to the dead. So
many times, I lost count. Whenever the world gets
me down, I come to the cemetery and hold onto the
stone. I just hold onto the cold hard stone for dear
life, as if it will save me from something. I don't know
what – something terrible. My Dad put one word on
my Momma's stone: wife. What about Mother?

Three movies – that's all I made, just three little
flicks: *Rebel*, *East of Eden*, and *Giant* – that's all! My
whole legend rests on three motion pictures. When
I was a kid, I dreamed of fame – not Hollywood as
such, just fame. I never thought it would be like this:
people staring at you in the street; stopping you in
the street; cutting you up in the car – Jeez! They must
be desperate! It's like living by proxy, through a
screen, through someone else!

People often wonder about me, my sexuality, who I
am, so! I had girlfriends, and I had boyfriends. Lots
of 'em. I'm not a freak, there are plenty of people
like me – the Twilight Folk! Guys and gals. Jonathan
Gilmore! He was one beautiful guy! Actor, good
looking. We fooled around. Once I grabbed his cock
through his pants, in a restaurant. Under the table!
He didn't dig that! We talked about everything:
acting, fucking other men, going with men. It was
all talk, no action with him. He was beautiful, but it

never worked out. He was too tight, uptight, tight-assed! I tried, but he couldn't take it, poor guy. I guess it just wasn't his time.

Time, that's what it's all about. Timing: split second precision. Timing: an actor's gift. If I could just cheat time by going fast enough, fast enough to break the sound barrier, fast enough to always stay young, to meet eternity – yes siree! To go fast enough to cheat on time – death can't be considered because if you're afraid of death, there's no room in life to make discoveries!

They can't kill me – those Hollywood Bastards! Cars. Love this car – my Spyder Porsche, the Little Bastard, that's what I called her, my baby! She killed me! 'Each man kills the things he loves', Oscar Wilde said that. But, things you love can kill you! Funny that! Things you love kill you in the end: drink, drugs, fast women, men. I died young…

I met this English actor once, Alec Guinness. Kinda straight, square, man! Does all the Shakespeare and stuff. He saw me standing by my car in LA, my Spyder Porsche, and he said the strangest thing: 'Do not get into the car', he said, 'I have a bad feeling about it.' Isn't that weird! The weirdest thing! Maybe he was psychic or something, almost like he knew what was coming. There's another thing I gotta tell, ya know? About a week before I died I had my picture taken in this coffin. Don't know why, just had this sudden urge to lie down in this coffin, have my picture taken. It was at Hunt's Funeral Parlour, where they fixed Momma for burial, made her look real pretty. I was on this photo shoot trying to get my face on the front cover of *Time* magazine when we came to Hunt's. I just got in and told them to 'shoot'! *Time* turned it down, bastards! Maybe all great actors are psychic, that's how we do what we do. We're very special people picked by God to be his clowns, and that is why they love us – our public. Razzle-dazzle them – I always do!

Beat bongo drums.

I wanna revolutionize the stage, I'm gonna create new art forms, a whole new style of acting. I'm gonna set the screen on fire. I'm a cock teaser, a clit teaser, everybody wants to fuck me – I FUCK NOBODY! I go home alone and jerk off. I mostly get stuck into my scripts, tell the truth, that's what I like best. Me and my lines, making the words my own, fresh, like you're saying them for the first time, like a new thought. I become the character I'm playing, I transform into whoever is up there on the screen. He explodes in my head and suddenly he's there. Like this guy I played in *Giant.* He doesn't dig Rock Hudson, no siree, he doesn't. So I'm mean to him, 24/7 I'm real mean to him, and it kinda gets Rock down. But that's the way things are between them. I really got to him. I burned him down, I burned down Rock Hudson! Jesus I was mean, but it worked! Look at how we bounce off each other on screen – like lightning! He hated me for real, but it got results! IT WORKS!

Stop bongos.

People are dumb. They need something to latch onto. It's because they're empty inside so they need something or somebody to look up to, to worship, to imitate. That's why they become film fans. Movies make them come alive again, they almost feel like they mean something, poor bastards! All of 'em sitting there lost and alone in the dark and then something happens. It's like the light of a star suddenly shines down on them and illuminates every

149

corner of their pitiful lives, and it's magic! They feel
the power of my fame, by proxy. It's almost like
praying and God appears and throws a handful of
stardust down on them. Fan magazines carry my
image, my picture is on every newspaper, fan clubs
spring up over night and take my name in vain. My
name that's on everybody's lips, those lips that would
like to devour me if I let them. They'd eat me whole,
eat me alive and tear me into pieces then swallow
me so I become their sacrament, their God! I'm alive
forever inside them, Dionysius: being torn apart
and reborn a thousand, million times in their little
galaxies...

I do anything to get what it takes, be what I want.
I piss people off! People say I'm all screwed up
– twisted. Let them think what they want. I'm a crazy
mixed-up kid – they think. Maybe it's true, perhaps
I am. Or is it just what I want them to think? I had
an okay childhood. Didn't like Dad, we never got
on, not after Mom died. But there is no excuse in my
background for the way I am. Guess there was a bad
seed somewhere along the line, deep in the blood.
Fucked up – that's me. Well and truly! Marilyn, she
said about me once: 'He is the only person more
fucked up than me!' Crazy bitch! But it's true, I am: a
crazy mixed-up kid! The rest are squares. All my life
I been misunderstood. It was hell, but at least in hell
you know you're alive, pain keeps you alive. Stifling
in my skin, suffocating. Like hot needles and pins.
You wanna jump out of that skin, inhabit another's
flesh, but the only way to do that is to fuck them and
that's not the answer. When it's over, it's just another
game. It means nothing, it's gone! You're born alone,
you live alone and you die alone. In the end you're
trapped in this stuff and the loneliness goes on and
on. I've left my body far behind me now, now it's just

dust, stardust. A mangled wreck after the car crash, I
was a mess, but I was messed up before on the inside
where it didn't show. Outside I was pretty enough.
Just as well people can't see in! It didn't take a steel
spike sticking through my flesh. I was messed up long
before that. My Daddy messed me up, and Mom
– dying like that. No wonder I love death.

I guess you could say I'm in love with Death, always
have been. You could say Death has always been on
my mind, yes. It's a little bit like love, romantic love,
Death. He always called to me seductively, like a
beautiful boy, he fascinated me.

Lying in that coffin I felt I knew what dying was like,
but I never had a real death-wish, not consciously.
Though perhaps somewhere I wanted to experience
everything: strangulation, suffocation. They say you
get a last powerful orgasm when you're hanged by
the neck. Yes, I guess death fascinated me always,
Death and the Maiden!

The city's strange, big scary neon. I'm just a small-
town boy from a hick town. Country boy, farm-hand,
that's me! I don't fit in anywhere. I call Brando,
tell him everything, he's my god! I'm hours on the
phone, talking to him, he's the nearest thing to a
father confessor. He always picks up the phone
and listens, but I think he's just laughing. He never
speaks, never answers my questions, but I know
he's hanging on the phone, listening and it makes
me feel less alone. I can hear him breathing, I feel
him thinking. Why won't he speak? Bastard! Talk to
me! Like God, he remains silent. Cities, artifice…
(Beat bongos.) There's people bought and sold in this
city like it's a butcher's shop, an abattoir! Buyers
and sellers eye each other up – like the meat market
hanging on a hook. That one's tasty, that one's got

too much fat, that one's lean and sinewy just like
being on the meat rack. Street traders evaluate your
worth, calculate your flesh. That's Hollywood, or
New York: anywhere there's meat. The name of the
game is: how tasty is your joint? Do you make a nice
cut?

They don't think I'm good enough, they laugh at
my accent. They think I'm just a hick – a small-town
boy! Guess I am. Fuck 'em! I'll show them. Those
mealy-mouthed motherfuckers! I'll show 'em what
I'm made of! I can do any role – anything! Just
gimme the chance, gimme a break some bastard!
BASTARDS! But of course they won't, unless I play
the right kinda games. There's a big homosexual
mafia in Hollywood. The big boys. Big men with big
cocks and big mouths. Powerful guys. You audition
for them and they size you up if you're pretty like
me. They eye you up and down like a piece of meat
while they're sucking on their big fat phallic cigars!
They look at you like you're something on the menu.
You stand in front of them and they say leaning
back in their big fat armchairs: 'Hey, Boy!' They
like to call you boy like you were some shoe shine
merchant, 'Hey, Boy! Before I can cast you kid, I like
to get to know my actors better! Know what I mean?'
I sure as shit know what that means. I read between
the lines. I smile and nod. Walk into the bedroom
and he kicks the door closed behind. Takes his jacket
off. I take off mine. We stand facing each other like
a couple of cats, or two cowboys having a standoff.
He approaches me and grabs my belt. Hard. 'Get my
drift boy?' 'Sure,' I say and give him a smile, more a
grin really, a knowing sorta grimace. And I sure as
hell get his drift. In my face. I've sucked dick and had
my dick sucked by some of the most powerful men in
Hollywood. Not naming names but take my word for

it. It opened lotsa doors when I was broke and down on my luck – desperate for a job, I'd do anything. I did anything. You have to make a choice and take that chance. Life here's too tough not to. You gotta work to eat right? I made the decision. Whatever it takes. I had to do it. I was an instant hit with what you might call the fist-fuck set. Up for anything – even if it hurt. They used boots, belts on me, and bondage. And cigarettes. Cigarette burns all over my flesh. They used my body to stub out cigarettes. Look! That's how I earned my nickname: The 'Human Ashtray', like this: *(Takes cigarette and burns.)* In time I got used to it. Hell! I even started to enjoy it! At least with pain you know you're alive!

First time I came to the end of a film, I was dog-tired – but elated too. I could feel it all happening – A STAR IS BORN! I went to the premiere of that film, cameras popping. I didn't go to the premiere of *East of Eden*, it was too much like my life in a way: a son trying to win his father's love. I never did make that breakthrough with my Dad. Kazan got it right. The minute he met my Dad he knew exactly what was going on. He sensed it. Steinbeck too! He got it right. 'He is Cal', he said when he met me. They sent me off to the desert to get a tan, I looked pale. So, I went to the desert, got a tan and put on a few pounds. With my first thousand bucks I bought a red MG, she was fast, she was fabulous, a real firecracker. They cast Raymond Massey as my Dad, he sure as hell was hard to work with. We clashed. He thought I was a heel, a dog! But I couldn't be any different. We just never hit it off. He was old school, never changed the lines, threw him if *I* did – and I changed the lines a lot. He HIT THE ROOF! I got myself a bad reputation for being difficult and it stuck like shit to a blanket.

Hollywood fanfare/White Out.

USA rules, OK? It's 1950, we're gods. It's the Land
of Opportunity! We dropped an A-bomb on Japan,
but hey, we're God's chosen country. And anybody
can be president, or a movie star! Me, I chose to be
a serious actor. But hey, what the hell! If Hollywood
calls, I'm free! It's the Land of Opportunity! I'm
picked for a Pepsi-Cola ad on TV and I stand out
– the director likes me. This leads onto lotsa other
things, and the director always likes me. That's when
they're not screaming at me for being difficult, being
late, being moody, not knowing my lines. They just
love me. But I always stand out in a crowd. I'm not
made of the stuff to be an extra. And they notice
me because I'm different. They dig the difference
too, but they don't know it yet. But they will. Those
bastards will love me – I'll make them fall in love
with me.

While people are still melting from the A-bomb
and forming grease pools on the streets of Nagasaki,
we're busy hatching the first teenage revolution
– not the one in 1968, the one after I was long dead
and gone, and never happened. The Prequel. The
mid 1950s teenage revolution – before 'teenagers'
were invented. America was one big self-satisfied
Mother! Greed and grab and get. McCarthy witch-
hunts were on. Names were named. A lot of actors
fell foul of that paranoia. It was an era of paranoia,
of suspicion. People like me, we could have gone to
the wall, I was a rebel, a Rebel Without A Cause. But
American Imperialism rules, OK. And it still does.
The American Dream had gone bad, and it's rotten
to the core.

In New York, I really explored myself. My sex,
always a mystery to others, Hell and to me! I had
affairs, not relationships, affairs… with a lot of men.
All sorts of men. Some rough trade and some not.
My boy dancer wasn't rough. Blue-eyed, blonde,
delicate. I used to go round and visit him just for
sex. It was amazing, no holes barred. No restraints!
Sometimes we'd do it in the open hallway on the
landing, I'd hold onto the door frame and he used to
take me right there – anyone coming in might catch
us. It added to the thrill, they'd have got an eyeful!
I pushed myself to the limit! There are no limits as
far as I'm concerned. I tried everything. And the
further I went the deeper my acting got. It gave me a
whole new dimension. I just got good at being inside
other people's heads. I gave all New York good head!
(Laugh.) People commented on my performance, I
explored more, got deeper into it. My potential was
fathomless…

Bar noise.

About this time I start living with Rogers Brackett,
older man with cash, and style. Cash opens doors,
style helps too. 1952, New York. Hanging out at the
Algonquin, sitting, sipping bourbon in the lounge
– I hated it! He liked me to do it, to show me off to
his friends, like a new lapdog! Bitchy queens! All
they talked about was who was doing what to who!
Boring! One night I counted fifteen names being
dropped! Fifteen! About fifty times! Sons of boring
bitches! All prominent queens on the scene. 'Sons
of boring bitches,' I kept muttering. Sons of bitches
all of them. Rogers didn't like that one little bit. So
he was keeping me, so what! YOU DON'T OWN
ME! NOBODY OWNS ME! But he introduced me

to a lot of his friends, influential man on the scene. I couldn't stand it for too long, had to move out, move on...

Guess I'm too tricky to live with. But this book Rogers gave to me, it was called *The Little Prince*. Like my Bible that book was, I read it over and over again, it became my credo. It's about this little guy from another planet who falls to Earth in the Sahara desert where he meets this pilot whose plane has crashed. But before that he meets a fox and the fox tells him a secret, a secret so precious that he whispers it and the secret is this: 'That it is only with the heart one can rightly see. What is essential is invisible to the naked eye.' I've lived by that credo all my life. The Little Prince who fell to Earth like a star, briefly lighting up the sky with gold. I didn't know it at the time, but that was me. I was that Little Prince. Just like a star that falls to Earth and dies before his time. A falling star, that's what I was, falling, falling, *(Crash.)* there! Another star lights up the firmament.

So, it's 1952 and I'm accepted into the Actors Studio in New York. God, that's a big break for a boy like me. I can't believe my luck, walking through those doors where all the greats have gone, and Lee Strasberg: Master of Ceremonies! 'You have a talent, but it is undisciplined. What you do is simple and believable, it has a wonderful quality', so far so good. But then it all turned sour like so many things in my life seem to do. I do a piece that I prepared for him, it was a last minute decision to change the scene and, boy, that one big mistake: 'It's crass! It's crap! Call that acting? Call that a performance? You oughta been a cowhand!', and on and on. He knocked the guts outta me. And an actor's gotta have guts, or what's left? I don't know what's inside but it's gotta come out when I act. I'm the first postmodern actor.

It's the truth. It's the goddamn truth! I create a style
that's all my own – in the moment, that's what it's all
about. Being in the moment! It's like making love:
you can't do it if you're somewhere else! Clift does it
quite a lot, and Brando too, pretty much all the time.
That's what I'm trying to do! To be TRUTHFUL
EVERY MOMENT! But Lee doesn't get it. He's
abusive, and I can't take it! Time to do the rounds,
endless knocking on unending doors, rejection after
rejection – that's something you gotta get used to
when you're an actor. It destroys your soul. I didn't
just knock, though, I hammered like hell! I got to cut
my teeth on other forms; I studied art; I even studied
dance; and of course I played the bongos…

The thing about Pier Angeli and me, we were a
match made in Hollywood heaven. Hell, even I
started to believe it for a time. I started to swallow
the Hollywood fanzine talk, because it was kinda
romantic for a guy like me, a guy who likes men, to
marry a pretty little thing like Pier. Who knows how
things may have worked out. It sure woulda been
different! Then perhaps maybe I wouldn't have died
and been a legend. Hell! Maybe we'd have kids. Son
of James Dean! I'd be fat, and fifty, and a mess! Hell
No! *(Song: 'Going to the Chapel'.)* She married Vic
Damone. Good, Catholic creep! Greaseball! Well,
good luck to 'em! *(Motorbike.)* There's a legend I went
roaring off on my motorbike outside the church, I
went off crying, that's the legend. Oh, it isn't true, but
I did drive hell for leather outta that town that day!
Pier, she was so beautiful, I didn't realise till it was
too late. Guess it did hurt me at the time. I got into
a black depression! So, I went out with a lot of guys
to get over the pain. All kindsa men! Hell! What did
it matter then? She didn't care what I was doing! I
missed her a lot, you can't forget someone by fucking

around, it doesn't work, memories hang around, the heart hurts at night, when you're cold and alone – even with a stranger beside you. You wish sometimes it was that person you knew so well, that person who was close and intimate with you in a different way from those men who just screw you and use you and then throw you away at dawn. But the dawn always comes up cold and you're alone even when you're with someone, some stranger you found prowling on the Boulevard of Broken Dreams, like the song…

Song: 'Boulevard of Broken Dreams'.

The loneliness – I scream inside my skin, inside my skull. There's nowhere so lonely as the big city. Busy people, coming and going. All of the them, all day long, with their busy little lives. 'We're busy doing nothing, but buzzing around like flies!' Sweet fuck nothings. I try and keep myself busy too: I take lessons in dancing with Eartha Kitt; I take classes – anything to keep the void at bay. The city never sleeps and neither do I. I haunt the bars, I hunt in the bars. You meet some strange insomniacs like yourself, hag-ridden, hollow-eyed, sleepwalkers in the twilight world, that in-between world. Sometimes I fuck 'em, sometimes I send 'em home. Alien encounters in the dead of night, but the neon is always bright, relentless, even in the dead of night. I walk the dark side of my inner soul. Close encounters of an intimate kind, that mean nothing. Sometimes, I watch two people fucking, I play the voyeur. I don't do anything. It's all part of my training, I tell myself, to break new ground with my acting technique. I tell myself it's all good experience. *(Laughs.)* All sortsa people get caught in my net: human detritus! Most of 'em I throw away with the dawn, but it stops the loneliness… sometimes…

Hi! Jimmy Dean! Yes sir, I brought a new piece
from a screenplay by a friend of mine – oh, you
don't wanna know what its called? Yeah, I play
this guy who's all screwed up, right… ok. I got
this thing, this illness, it's inherited, ya see. My
Daddy was a no good bastard so he gave me this
disease, it's congenital, it's in my blood, it's not my
fault, I inherited it and, and… No, it's not right,
I'd like to start again, I think I got some words
wrong – I'M TRYING TO GIVE A TRUTHFUL
PERFORMANCE HERE, GODDAMMIT! Sorry!
I just wanna try again, I'm just getting into it now,
give me a minute! I need more time. No, I am not
wasting the studio's valuable time! Do you want
a real performance by a real actor or just some
manufactured shit? No! I'm sorry! What? Aw, shit,
have it your own way! You don't want me to do the
speech again? Well, FUCK YOU THEN! That's how
it was: that's how I was! I took no prisoners, took no
shit! Self-obsessed me to the bitter end. A bastard,
but, it takes one to know one and bastards make the
best actors!

The job I finally landed was in *The Immoralist* by
André Gide. Great role for me! I played this Arab
houseboy, homosexual called Bachir, who seduced
his master. Great part. Though I had trouble with the
director and the actor Louis Jourdan, they thought
they knew it all! But I showed them, just when I
was about to talk I cracked it in a big way with the
famous scissor dance! It made my name, I hit all the
headlines! The critics loved me – I was their darling,
just for once! That famous, infamous scissor dance!
You wanna see it? Watch: I'll show you what all the
fuss was about!

Scissor Dance to Salome.

Yeah, they certainly all loved it! But then, at the very height of my fame, I quit! I handed in my two weeks' notice. They were stunned: they didn't know why. But I did! It was because at that time Elia Kazan called my agent and offered me the role of Cal in *East of Eden*. Now, I wasn't gonna turn down a lead role in Hollywood just to be on Broadway, now was I? Hold the bus!

Hollywood Fanfare.

Hollywood! Tinseltown! Casual encounters were all I had to fill my empty life. My days were full, but my nights… were never-ending. So, enter Jack Simmons, my sometime lover. He was very devoted, jeez! He even tried to change his looks to be like me: he had a nose job! Even dressed the same. Like twins! That was quite something, like living with a mirror image. Making love to him was just like jacking off! He was determined and told all his friends: 'I'm gonna be with Jimmy Dean long term!' And he did, for a long time. He copied me, it was weird, man! That cat was something. He kept a pair of my boots in a glass case, like a shrine! He made a holy relic out of my body! One time, he hit on my old time love Jonathan Gilmour, but they never got in on, just jacked off or something! Weird, huh?

But I didn't care! I was a star by then, by that time James Dean had arrived. The whole world knew my name. I was interviewed by all the press.

Mr. Harold Thompson, *New York Times*, pleased to meet you sir. No sir, I never did read the novel of *East of Eden*, I prefer the adaptation. Yeah, I felt I understood the part, if I had a problem, Kazan would set me straight. Strasberg? Incredible man, a walking encyclopaedia. New York? Love it! I feel in cadence here, as far as living goes. New York is vital and, above all, fertile. Out there in Hollywood, behind all that glass, there are people who are just as sensitive to things too. The only problem for this cat, me, is not to get too lost! No, no, I didn't go to the premiere of *East of Eden* – too much pressure. Death? Well, it can't be considered, because, like I said before, if you're afraid to die, there's no room in life to make discoveries. Strictly off the cuff, I've had my cock sucked by five of the biggest names in Hollywood. But hey, Hollywood's no place for a fag, which is funny cos it's full of them and I wanted, more than anything on this Earth, to get some little part, to do something. And they'd invite me to dinner overlooking the ocean and give me drinks and how long could I go on holding out? That's what I want to know! And the answer was that it could go on until there was nothing left, until they had what they wanted and there was nothing left – just one big fat zero! Miss Parson, pleased to meet you! Please sit down! Best behaviour with this one, Louella can make and break reputations! Yes ma'am, truth is: I'm dog-tired. Three pictures, back to back almost. I need a rest! Yeah, they say I've done the Hollywood thing, but the truth is, I'm exactly the same as when I didn't have a dime. I need a break! Yes Ma'am, pleasure to meet you too. Phew! That's one mean mother! No, no more questions. Romance? Pier and me? Yeah, we're very good friends. Marry? Who knows, we'll see what happens. Engaged? I'm saying nothing, who knows, we're still very young. Now, get out of here!

I guess if it could be any woman, it would be her: Pier, my angel. She could have saved me from death, but not from fame. And then where would my legend be? On some faded cutting-room floor full of dreams. And I like my ambiguity, it's part of me. No, best leave things the way they are. Keep away from Pier, don't destroy her. No, Pier, I loved you in my own way, it's true, but you must be gone! Demon woman! That's how the fanzine painted her: the Girl Who Broke James Dean's Heart! But if she'd known about me it would have destroyed her! And I didn't want that to happen. Now we're just another Hollywood romance, another legend. We are the stuff of dreams.

My ma, she died when I was young. I was only nine, guess I never really got over it. I still miss her, it's like part of your life is empty, missing something, don't know exactly what. Like losing a limb. You go to reach out for her and she's not there. There's this... absence. A void. Something's gone, just gone forever from my life like a light being switched off in a room that's familiar until the light has gone, then suddenly you're blind. You think you know your way around, but suddenly you're bumping into everything. It's weird. I can't remember her so good anymore. Sometimes I try to picture her, close my eyes and go back in time. It's hard. And the further away in time, the further her image fades. Sometimes, I can't even recall her voice, but then there are other times when I almost catch a glimpse of her, like a shadow on the wall from my dreams, like a ghost, just flickering, in the corner of my eye across the room and then... she's gone. Once I thought I heard her voice, calling my name. The dead can't come back and talk to us can they? If they can, then I'm glad to go over and be with my mom. She's there, teaching me how to draw and paint. Teaching me how to speak all those poems she knew by heart and loved. Showing me dance steps. Oh, Momma loved to dance. She was so graceful, like a swan. She was something my mother. I take after her, artistic, like her.

There's this story I told you before – about The Little
Prince who fell to the Earth. That's me. That's like
my story. I was the Little Prince that fell to the Earth.
I'm still falling and all the days of my life I strive to
be like him. Like a star that falls to Earth and then is
gone. Or a meteor that blazes up brightly and leaves
a shining streak in the sky. A comet leaves a silver
trail behind that never dies, but goes on through the
cosmos forever, gets absorbed by the astral dust. Star!
That's the Little Prince. Forever young and beautiful,
like a fairy tale, never grow old. That's the secret: live
fast, die young. And I am him. I wanted to film his
story, to be him on the screen but maybe I already
am him. I wanted to make his life into a film, this
book that I have loved and lived with for so long,
but unless someone else comes along, that's a book
that will never be filmed, because it's mine and now
I'm so long gone they've forgotten – oh, not about
me! There are still plenty of fans in pursuit of their
own death ride, but they've forgotten HIM. The
Little Prince. It's like Sleeping Beauty, waiting for
the Prince's kiss. She waited a long time, a hundred
years. I'll kiss that little prince someday and wake
him up again, meantime I have to live with what
happened – hear that sound? *(Crash.)* Again and
again! Somebody must wake him into new life again,
from beyond the grave. Somebody, anybody, please
help! Somebody come and kiss the Little Prince, he's
still there somewhere. Somewhere like an embryo,
waiting for that kiss, just waiting to be born.

The End.

www.ingramcontent.com/pod-product-compliance
Ingram Content Group UK Ltd.
Pitfield, Milton Keynes, MK11 3LW, UK
UKHW020721280225
455688UK00012B/460